*Democratic Capitalism
and Its Discontents*

Democratic Capitalism and Its Discontents

Brian C. Anderson

ISI Books

Wilmington, Delaware

2007

Anderson, Brian C.

    Democratic capitalism and its discontents / Brian C. Anderson. – 1st ed. – Wilmington, DE : ISI Books, c2007.

        p. ; cm.

        ISBN-13: 978-1-933859-24-8
        ISBN-10: 1-933859-24-5
        Includes index.

        1. Capitalism. 2. Political science. 3. Political science—Philosophy.

HB501 .A53 2007   2007923889
330.12/2–dc22   0706

Published in the United States by:
ISI Books
Intercollegiate Studies Institute
Post Office Box 4431
Wilmington, DE 19807-0431
wwww.isibooks.org

Book design by Kara Beer
Manufactured in the United States of America

Contents

III. Recto/Verso

Preface

In March 2007, Benjamin Barber, the Gershon and Carol Kest Professor of Civil Society at the University of Maryland, released *Consumed: How Markets Corrupt Children, Infantilize Adults, and Swallow Citizens Whole*. Published by Norton, the book generated a lot of media buzz; the author even appeared on the hip *faux* news program *The Colbert Report*. *Consumed*'s subtitle nicely captures its argument: American-style democratic capitalism is ruining everything, from the National Basketball Association to civic responsibility. If left unchecked by political action—including something called a "democratized globalization"—it will culminate in a totalitarian "ethos of induced childishness," and maybe the end of democracy and capitalism themselves. Barber, author of earlier works on "strong democracy" and Rousseau, is a man of the hard Left. What might have surprised some observers is that a lengthy excerpt from his book became a cover story in the *American Conservative*, a hard-Right magazine founded by Patrick Buchanan.

It is this hostility to the free market on the left and even on part of the right that I try to understand and assess in this book. Despite defeating its fiercest ideological opponents (communism, fascism, and National Socialism), and despite generating unprecedented prosperity, democratic capitalism still faces existential challenges in the new millennium. Not only has a fanatical form of Islam shattered the peace of the postcommunist era; Western societies remain troubled, even threatened, by internal discontents: egalitarian fantasies, moral libertinism, an arid secularism, and a "suicide" of culture, evident in many of our elite educational institutions. Yet none of these problems is a fate accompli. This book is a defense of democratic capitalism. But I give it (as Irving Kristol or Michael Novak have done) only two cheers, since it's the most imperfect of social orders—except for all the others.

The book's opening section, "The Bourgeois Prospect," considers the cultural and economic arguments against capitalism and globalization. Against anticapitalist leftists such as one-time terror master Antonio Negri, I conclude that globalization is ultimately beneficial, and indeed is the only way we know to lift humanity out of poverty. The conservative argument that unleashed free markets necessarily lead to a nihilist libertinism, as seen in the worst aspects of American popular culture, is also wrong. The connection between nihilism and capitalism is accidental, resulting from the betrayal of culture by many of our elites. (I confess, too, that conservative arguments against the degraded aspects of our popular culture seem less pressing to me after 9/11; if it comes to a choice between Britney and the burka, I'll go with the Pop Tart.)

Part Two, "The American Difference," looks at the democratic capitalist nation par excellence, a county which I believe has most successfully approximated the bourgeois ideal. The United States differs from other liberal democracies in its religiosity, its vigorous civil society, and its remarkable history of constitutionalism, all of which has unified a diverse nation and helped make it both powerful and free. These achievements are under threat from the Left, which promotes by contrast an aggressive secularism, an overweening state, and a transformation of constitutional law into partisan politics.

The book's final section, "Recto/Verso," explores the work of various leading political thinkers, on the left and right, who have sought either to revolutionize or radically transform democratic capitalism in order to create an egalitarian society (Jean-Paul Sartre and John Rawls), or else to understand democratic capitalism and perhaps elevate it, or at least preserve its decencies (John Kekes, Bertrand de Jouvenel, Marcel Gauchet, and Pierre Manent). A secondary argument in these chapters concerns how to think politically. Too often, contemporary political philosophy is hopelessly abstract, developing theoretical models cut off from the real concerns and passions of human beings, from history, from human nature, and from what we know about institutional life. The handful of writers whom I here treat sympathetically avoid that error.

Much of the material in these pages has been substantially reworked and updated from essays that first appeared in several publications: *First Things* (chapters 1, 2, 9, and part of 10); the late, lamented *Public Interest* (chapters 4, 6, 7, and part of 10); my own magazine *City Journal* (chapter 5); *Policy Review* (chapter 8); and *National Review* (part of chapter 10). Chapter 3 is based on research begun under the auspices of the Acton Institute. I want to thank the editors of these magazines and organizations for their advice and suggestions (and for permission to draw on my previously published work here), especially my friend and colleague Myron Magnet, Fr. Richard John Neuhaus, Adam Wolfson, Tod Lindberg, and Mike Potemra.

Other thanks: ISI's Jeremy Beer, for his unfailing enthusiasm and excellent editorial direction in pushing this book to completion; my employer, the Manhattan Institute, and its president Larry Mone, for providing such a hospitable–and exciting–environment for ideas; *City Journal*'s Ben Plotinsky for his help in organizing my affairs, freeing time for me to write; my *CJ* colleagues Steven Malanga and Nicole Gelinas; Lindsay Craig and Clarice Smith of the crack MI communications team; my agent Andrew Stuart; Daniel J. Mahoney; my parents Chuck and Theresa; and above all my wonderful wife Amy and our two boys, Luke and Nick, who always make it tough to work, since I just want to have fun with them.

Democratic Capitalism and Its Discontents is dedicated to Michael Novak, whom I worked for at the American Enterprise Institute for three fast-paced years, from 1994 through late 1997. Michael has thought longer and harder than anyone– and with great practical effect–about democratic capitalism and its possibilities.

I. The Bourgeois Prospect

1

Capitalism and the Suicide of Culture

Not long before he died, the political philosopher Isaiah Berlin somberly summed up his, and our, age: "I have lived through most of the twentieth century without . . . suffering personal hardship. I remember it only as the most terrible century in Western history." What made it so terrible is politics—or, more precisely, the secular religions of National Socialism and communism, which violently sought to transfigure the bourgeois economic and political condition of modern man. The exact number of people killed by these political adventures will never be known, but it exceeds 125 million.

Those secular religions are now gone, leaving behind only ruin. Communism, as an ongoing political experiment, expired with the collapse of the Berlin Wall in 1989; National Socialism didn't survive the crushing military defeat delivered by the Allies in World War II. In the early days of the twenty-first century, it is difficult to imagine a serious ideological challenger to what communism and National Socialism wanted to destroy: prosaic bourgeois liberal democracy—what others call democratic capitalism.

Despite the fall of these political messianisms, however, the future of democratic capitalism is by no means unclouded, and not just because of the very serious physical threat posed by radical Islam, which some see as itself a new form of ideological politics. The hubris of the secular religions was to think that they had solved "the political problem." Properly understood, democratic capitalism makes no such claims. It has been a virtue of the richest current of liberal democratic thought, from James Madison and Alexis de Tocqueville to Irving Kristol and Pierre Manent, to explore bourgeois society's inherent limitations and failings without losing sight of its basic decency and relative justness.

The work of three leading contemporary thinkers—none of them on the conventional left—enables us to confirm the relevance of that anti-utopian tradition and gain a better understanding of what troubles democratic capitalism today.

The Dream of Transcending Politics

We begin with the late French historian François Furet, who provides striking insights into the political tensions of democratic capitalism. At the time of his death in 1997, Furet was France's foremost historian and the world's preeminent authority on the French Revolution. Though once a Marxist himself, Furet broke with the Marxist view of the French Revolution—long dominant in French historiography—which saw it as an economically determined bourgeois warm-up for the Russian Revolution of October 1917. In the Marxian optic, 1789 was the inevitable result of a rising bourgeoisie overthrowing the ancien régime and the agricultural society that it represented. Furet, however, rejected the notion of historical inevitability and gave human political actions a central explanatory role. In a Tocquevillian register of conservative liberalism, he also claimed that the revolution had released utopian hopes for a humanity at last reconciled with itself and in control of its destiny, hopes that neither liberal democracy nor any other political regime, including socialism, could ever satisfactorily fulfill.

In *The Passing of an Illusion: The Idea of Communism in the Twentieth Century*, which appeared in France in 1995 and quickly became a controversial bestseller across Europe, Furet shifted his focus to the twentieth century and specifically to the rise and decline of the communist dream, the shape finally taken by those profound but—when directed into politics—destructive longings first unleashed by the French revolutionaries. Disabused, attentive to the complex interactions of "ideas, intentions, and circumstances" that give meaning to history, Furet's final testament was written on the far side of the revolutionary passions of the epoch. It serves as a kind of warning: we must not expect too much from politics.

Communism's seductive appeal, Furet argues, came in considerable part from its coupling of the inherently incompatible ideas of human volition and the science of history. The Bolsheviks showed the true capacity of man's revolutionary will, which, in the most backward nation of Europe, promised the achievement of human liberation first announced by the French Revolution. To this "cult of volition," Furet explains, "Lenin would add the certainties of science, drawn from Marx's *Capital.*" History has a predetermined outcome and, thanks to Marxist "science," we know exactly what it is, the revolutionaries claimed. Knowledge would transform proletarian man into the lord of time, ushering in the classless society.

It was never clear how a science of historical inevitability could be reconciled with the allegedly Promethean will that forged the Russian Revolution, but no matter. Berlin de-

5

scribes the emotional lure: "There is a curious human feeling that if the stars in their courses are fighting for you, so that your cause will triumph, then you should sacrifice yourself in order to shorten the process, to bring the birth pangs of the new order nearer." Will and science: "By combining these two supremely modern elixirs with their contempt for logic," Furet stringently notes, "the revolutionaries of 1917 had finally concocted a brew sufficiently potent to inebriate militants for generations to come."

Yet, however intoxicating communism's blend of revolutionary will and pseudoscience, it inebriated as many as it did because it both grew out of and exploited two fundamental political weaknesses of the bourgeois regime. The first weakness: liberal democracy had set loose an egalitarian spirit that it could never fully tame. The notion of the universal equality of man, which liberal democracy claims as its foundation, easily becomes subject to egalitarian overbidding. Equality constantly finds itself undermined by the freedoms that the liberal order secures. The liberty to pursue wealth, to seek to better one's condition, to create, to strive for power or achievement–all these freedoms unceasingly generate inequality, since not all people are equally gifted, equally nurtured, equally hardworking, equally lucky. Equality works in democratic capitalist societies like an imaginary horizon, forever retreating as one approaches it.

Communism professed to fulfill the democratic promise of equality. Real liberty could only be the achievement of a more equal world–a world, that is, *sans* bourgeoisie. And if what the communists derisively called the "formal" liberties of expression and political representation had to be sacrificed in order to establish the true freedom of a classless society, well, so be it. Thus was the "egalitarian apocalypse" set in motion, as Furet observes.

The second weakness of liberal democracy is more complex, though its consequences are increasingly evident: liberal democracy's moral indeterminacy. The "bourgeois city," as Furet terms it, is morally indeterminate because, basing itself on the sovereign individual, it constitutes itself as a rebellion against, or at least as a downplaying of, any extra-human or ontological dimension that might provide moral direction to life. For all the inestimable benefits of the bourgeois city—its threefold liberation, in Michael Novak's formulation, from tyranny, from the oppression of conscience, and from the pervasive material poverty of the premodern world—its deliverance from the past has come at a price.

Furet suggests that as the "self" moves to the center of the bourgeois world, existential questions—what is man? what is the meaning of life?—become difficult to answer. Communism, usurping the role of religion in checking the individualizing excesses of democratic modernity, falsely promised to resolve such pressing existential questions by providing a political articulation—horribly perverse, as it turned out—of human ends.

The two political weaknesses of the bourgeois order have their psychological corollaries: self-doubt and self-hatred. The bourgeois man finds himself unsettled by a guilty conscience and spiritual dissatisfaction. "Self-doubt," Furet writes, "has led to a characteristic of modern democracy probably unique in universal history, the infinite capacity to produce offspring who detest the social and political regime into which they were born—hating the very air they breathe, though they cannot survive without it and have known no other." Hatred of the bourgeoisie, on the right as well as the left, is a tale as old as modernity itself, of course, but it is jarring to reflect on how much ire has come not from aristocratic revenants or fiery proles, but from the cerebral sons of businessmen. Historian Perry Anderson points out that most leading Marxist thinkers originally came from bourgeois money: Theodore Adorno, Walter Benjamin, Friedrich Engels, Lenin, Rosa Luxemburg, Herbert Marcuse, even Marx himself—all had fathers who were bankers, bureaucrats, lawyers, manufacturers, or merchants.

The end of World War I—a bourgeois war motivated by bourgeois concerns and supported by the bourgeois class—left middle-class Europe exhausted. Into the breach stepped the Soviet Union, the antibourgeois society with all the answers. In the interwar years, liberal democratic societies seemed powerless to control their fate, while the Soviet Union's "five-year plans," constructing the socialist future, appeared to many as models of human rationality. But as credible reports of purges, political terror, and starvation began to leak from Stalin's totalitarian netherworld during the 1930s, doubts about the communist system began to arise.

The chaotic aftermath of the Great War also spurred the rise of fascism, a second and rival critique of bourgeois modernity. Where communism embraced the universal ideals of 1789, fascism drew its revolutionary force from the ideal of the nation and—with its darkest star, National Socialism—racial ideology, making it what Furet calls the "pathology of the particular." Although professed mortal enemies, communism and fascism shared many affinities, including a loathing of the bourgeoisie.

Despite the failures of communism and fascism, the political weaknesses of the democracies—their susceptibility to egalitarian overbidding and their moral indeterminacy—are with us still. Nor are we free from hatred of the bourgeoisie; it remains virulent in both high and popular culture. The liberal democratic regime, by its very nature, observes Furet, "creates the need for a world beyond the bourgeoisie and beyond Capital, a world in which a genuine human community can flourish"—a need, he persuasively shows, that will never be met. With the fall of communism, "The idea of *another* society has become almost impossible to conceive of, and no one in the world today is offering any advice on the subject or even trying to formulate a new concept." "Here we are, condemned to live in the world as it is."

Is this strange antinomy of the human political condition—between the utopian impulse and prosaic reality—sustainable? Though communism and fascism have exited the stage of history, one should resist the temptation to conclude that the history of politics culminates in the bourgeois regime. New political monsters may yet arise from the unstable and ultimately dissatisfying bourgeois world. (The threat of Islamic radicalism is less an internal than an external challenge to that world, in my view.) More likely, liberal democratic societies will struggle with a generalized moral nihilism that is subversive of the social order, a concern I will return to later. In any case, the task of political thought is to guard against these threats, whatever shape they might take, through what Furet terms "the sad analysis of reality."

Economic Globalization: Bane or Boon?

If the political future of democratic capitalism remains uncertain, requiring both vigilance and reconciliation to this-worldly imperfections, what about its economic prospect? Though communism now rests in history's dustbin, anticapitalism is not without its influential adherents. Chief among them, perhaps, is the British political theorist John Gray. Gray is no traditional leftist. But having moved from Margaret Thatcher's camp in the 1980s to become a fierce critic of Thatcher's legacy during the 1990s, he is certainly no longer the free-market conservative he once was. His book *False Dawn,* published in 1998, along with other recent writings constitute blistering assaults on the global capitalism of competitive free markets, fast-moving entrepreneurs, and volatile stock exchanges.

In *False Dawn* Gray dismisses the assumption that global capitalism will spread wealth across the planet. Inverting Montesquieu's dictum, "Commerce . . . polishes and softens barbarian ways," Gray believes that capitalism is leading inexorably to a new, late-modern barbarism. Indeed, he argues, the project of creating a world market is as utopian as was Soviet communism—he stresses that both are Enlightenment ideologies wedded to the cult of reason and blind to history— and could ultimately "rival it in the suffering that it inflicts."

For Gray, the project for a world market is utopian because it seeks to transplant a U.S.-forged "unfettered" capitalism, characterized by flexible labor markets, low taxes, spirited competition, and relatively restrained welfare benefits, to cultures with radically different, "embedded" markets in which man's desire to barter and trade is constrained. The transplant will never take, he concludes, since unfettered markets are humanly unsatisfying. But global capitalism's "gale of creative destruction"—Gray borrows the language, though not the sobriety, of economist Joseph Schumpeter— will erode social cohesion by destroying settled ways of life, ignite fundamentalist movements (including Islamist ones) that will struggle to restore order by force, and lead rival powers to exploit natural resources ruthlessly until the earth is left cracked and barren. The world will face the "return of history, with its familiar intractable conflicts, tragic choices, and ruined illusions."

Gray paints global capitalism in lurid colors. "Already it has resulted in over a hundred million peasants becoming migrant laborers in China, the exclusion from work and participation in society of tens of millions in the advanced societies, a condition of near-anarchy and rule by organized crime in parts of the post-Communist world, and further devastation of the environment." In the United States, where the market is most free and its unyielding logic most visible, the technological innovation and cutthroat competition that characterize the creative destruction of capitalism have "proletarianized" the middle classes by eliminating stable careers and suppressing income growth, undermined the family, bred resentment over fast-rising inequality, and pushed innumerable uprooted and alienated individuals into criminality. Gray predicts that the dismal realities of the American economy will soon consume the world. Supporting his contention, he interprets the 1990s crisis of Asian capitalism as a harbinger of a "fast-developing crisis of global capitalism," a sign that global free markets have become ungovernable.

Gray sees no truly viable political response to global capitalism. He hopes for what one might call "market pluralism," the flourishing of varied kinds of market economies within different cultural and political forms. But his hope burns dimly, since he foresees no world power encouraging such a vision. The United States is the global market's chief sponsor, while socialism is dead, acknowledges Gray, and for good reason: "The legacy of socialist central planning has been ruinous." But Gray thinks that his preferred kind of "social democracy" has also gone into "final retreat," unable to resist the capitalist storm. Global markets, obeying a "New Gresham's Law" in which bad forms of capitalism drive out good, punish governments that borrow too much money or boost taxes to achieve full employment. A "race to the bottom" ensues, with governments stripping away social protections in order to remain economically competitive, and firms relocating to whatever global backwaters offer the cheapest labor costs.

This is a bleak picture. Fortunately, it's also fantasy. Gray's description of contemporary capitalism is wildly exaggerated. He overestimates the degree of the historical ascendancy of American-style capitalism as well as the destructive effects of economic globalization. Market pluralism is, in fact, a fairly accurate way of describing the global economy, and it is likely to remain so. To the "unfettered" capitalism of the United States—itself a caricature, since the American economy is heavily regulated—we can contrast Japanese capitalism, which still features long-term employment and tight relations between banks and other firms; the German social-market model, with generous welfare benefits, powerful trade unions, and high taxes; and the touted "Third Way" of Tony Blair's Labour Party in England. One needn't stake a claim on the merits of any particular brand of capitalism to grasp the reality of market pluralism.

Each kind of capitalism entails unavoidable trade-offs. German worker protections, for example, come at a cost: weak job growth and high unemployment. The freer market of the United States has led to booming job growth and low unemployment but greater disparities in wealth. Economic globalization, *pace* Gray, hasn't made these difficult social choices irrelevant. It does, however, punish exceedingly foolish economic programs, like François Mitterrand's 1981 nationalization of large swaths of the French private sector, which sent $3 billion a day in capital rushing from the country until his government was forced to change course. We may be witnessing the "final retreat" of extreme forms of social democracy, though even that it is doubtful—witness the rise of Hugo Chavez in Venezuela. Moreover, the pull of egalitarianism will always be powerful in democratic societies. Contrary to Gray, more regulated versions of capitalism than the American model remain viable, albeit at the cost of low job growth and high taxes. There is no wide-ranging "race to the bottom."

Only on two counts does Gray's economic analysis deserve deeper scrutiny. First, capitalism does tend to erode career stability, and the United States, where the project to establish the global market originated, is the best place to measure the insecurity creative destruction brings with it. "In their ever greater dependency on increasingly uncertain jobs," contends Gray, "the American middle classes resemble the classic proletariat of nineteenth-century Europe." In America today, he writes, the prospect of a career is becoming obsolete.

That overstates the situation. Many people still have long-term, even lifetime, careers. The employment turnover rate in America has shifted in the direction of mobility, but more because individuals are willingly changing jobs (or even careers) than because they are being fired or laid off. Nevertheless, there is some truth to Gray's contention. For much of the post–World War II period, technological changes came relatively slowly. Industry in the developed world grew used to fixed ways of doing things. Now, as competition from an increasingly international economy liberates ever more creativity and technological innovation, the insecurity of employees will continue to grow as whole industries become redundant and are replaced with new industries, some of them entirely unimagined just a short time before.

How much call is there today for vinyl record albums or typewriters, except as boutique curiosities? Who knows what new industries lie just beyond the horizon? Philosopher Rocco Buttiglione predicts that in the future we will have myriad "work opportunities" but fewer lifetime "jobs." Flexibility will be the key to prosperity, both nationally and individually.

Though we shouldn't exaggerate its extent, this economic transformation, inseparable from global capitalism's creative destruction, can lead to a social weakness comparable to democratic capitalism's political weaknesses of moral indeterminacy and radical egalitarianism. Some people will have a hard time adapting to the more flexible work world. Not everyone, after all, is cut out to be one of Tom Wolfe's Masters of the Universe. A life of constant anxiety about one's future would be, for some, a diminished life. Political thinkers need to think imaginatively about how to reduce such insecurity.

One option, however, is a dead end, and that is an expansive welfare state. Social democracy, at least in its extreme forms, massively swells the state, makes government power omnipresent, and drains economic life of its vitality. Unfortunately, some on the left still don't see, perhaps will never see, what Irving Kristol has described as the welfare state's "spreading spiritual malaise." Writing in 1840, Alexis de Tocqueville imagined

> a society consumed with such a malaise, in which government, compassionate toward its subjects, provides for their security, foresees and supplies their necessities, facilitates their pleasures, manages their principal concerns, directs their industry, makes rules for their testaments, and divides their inheritances. . . . It does not break men's will, but softens, bends, and guides it; it seldom enjoins, but often inhibits action; it does not destroy anything, but prevents much being born; it is not at all tyrannical, but it hinders, restrains, enervates, stifles, and stultifies so much that in the end each nation is no more than a flock of timid and hardworking animals with government as its shepherd.

Tocqueville's tutelary despotism, a world without risk or human excellence, is the end toward which Mitterandesque social democracy tends. It solves the problem of insecurity at the cost of restricting initiative.

More promising are the recommendations put forth by Michael Novak in his book *Business as a Calling: Work and the Examined Life*. First, Novak argues, policymakers should move to establish personal ownership of benefit packages (especially health care benefits, which companies carry only by historical accident) that can move from job to job with a worker should he be displaced by capitalism's creative destruction or choose a new career path. Second, as a way of combating labor's decline in an era of flexible economies, Novak proposes that visionary unions reconstitute themselves as independent business corporations, supplying trained workers, as needed, to other firms. Neither of these suggestions would eliminate insecurity, but they would be pragmatic, nonutopian ways of lessening the anxiety an open economy causes while preserving its opportunity-creating dynamism.

A more flexible economy also will require new habits, and new ways of teaching them. As Buttiglione writes: "People must learn to learn, but not learn just technical knowledge, because this changes easily." Individuals must be willing and able to adapt. If once one knew how to make vinyl albums, one must learn today how to operate the machines that make compact discs; and tomorrow, one will probably have to learn to do something else, as technology continues to evolve. Europe's stagnating welfare states have been, for decades now, more intent on consuming than creating wealth. Those nations, especially, require the kind of educational renewal called for by Buttiglione which will again make work a central virtue in democratic societies.

Responsible thought—Furet's sad analysis of reality—also has, then, a key role to play in the economic realm. It must weigh the plusses and minuses of the plurality of market models. And it must seek to temper the disadvantages of each. The market, we need to remember, is an instrument; we can always try to make it more effective in securing human flourishing. It functions as an Enlightenment ideology comparable with communism—as a secular religion, in effect—only if profit becomes a society's sole deity. Even in free-wheeling contemporary America, things aren't anywhere close to that. But democratic capitalism's economics, like its politics, are imperfect. This is as true as it has ever been in the age of global capitalism, which promises to make us at once more prosperous and more anxious, and thus constantly beckons tutelary despotism as an answer to our fears.

The Cultural Contradictions of Democratic Capitalism

Gray makes another argument, an old one, which has always shadowed bourgeois society. The free market, he claims, is incompatible with traditional forms of life and leads to a culture of anomic individualism, family disintegration, and social upheaval. Agreeing with Gray, at least in part, is Francis Fukuyama, author of the justly famous *The End of History and the Last Man* (1992), which argued that man's political history had reached its terminus in bourgeois liberal democracy.

In his 1999 book *The Great Disruption*, Fukuyama blames the social chaos of the post-sixties democratic world—spiraling crime, rising divorce, sky-high abortion and illegitimacy rates, and declining levels of trust and citizenship activities—on the transition from an industrial to a postindustrial economy. "Was it just by accident," he asks, "that these negative social trends, which together reflected weakening social bonds and common values holding people together in Western societies, occurred just as economies in those societies were making the transition from the industrial to the information era?" The "Great Disruption," in Fukuyama's telling, is the tainted fruit of the economic trends of the past three decades.

What was it, though, about the postindustrial economy that led to such negative consequences? First, says Fukuyama, we experienced a transformation in the nature of work. In the industrial era, most work was labor intensive. Men were more suited to it than women, simply because of their greater physical strength. But the postindustrial economy "substitutes information for material product." In an information economy, instead of the brawny assembly-line autoworker getting big rewards, it's the brainy programmer designing the car's computer system who draws the sizable salary.

Such far-reaching change in the reality of work opened the way for women to flood the workforce. Their competition with men for jobs put extraordinary pressure on the family by, among other things, diminishing the father's traditional role as breadwinner. Fukuyama notes that the decline of the traditional family correlates with many of the social pathologies, including crime, that have afflicted economically advanced Western societies since the sixties. Intensifying the strain on the family, he continues, was a technological invention of the postindustrial era: the Pill. The Pill encouraged the liberation of women from the constraints of the hearth, Fukuyama emphasizes. But it also altered men's attitudes by separating sex from childrearing obligations. Men's ties to family life, always more fragile than women's, since they have a more tenuous natural bond with their offspring, became even more precarious.

The postindustrial economy drives the Great Disruption in a second way, Fukuyama suggests (and here his argument exactly mirrors that of both Gray and sociologist Daniel Bell, who in several classic writings of the 1970s explored the "cultural contradictions of capitalism"). The breathtaking innovation of the information economy, and the kaleidoscope of choices it allows, "spills over" into moral and social norms, corroding authority and weakening the bonds of family, neighborhood, and nation. When I can choose from one hundred different breakfast cereals, Fukuyama implies, having one hundred different sexual partners does not seem especially unusual. The new, postindustrial bazaar allowed us to begin to choose our moralities, our pasts, and even our sexualities. Faced with such individualizing forces, the moral order cracked.

All this makes the end of history sound very unsatisfying. Not to worry, says Fukuyama: the Great Reconstruction has begun. Man cannot live with such anarchy for long. His social nature and his self-interested reason lead him to "renorm" social life, to invent new moral rules for getting along with his fellows. Furthermore, the ongoing turbulence of the postindustrial economy itself encourages the reemergence of social norms—or "social capital," as Fukuyama calls it. "A modern, high-tech society," he writes, "cannot get along without [social norms] and will face considerable incentives to produce them." We're already seeing the signs of the new order, Fukuyama notes: safer streets as crime drops, falling illegitimacy and divorce rates, an increase in the level of neighborly trust. (*City Journal*'s Kay S. Hymowitz has dubbed this trend "Morning After in America.") Fukuyama draws on game theory and a formidable range of recent research in the life sciences, including evolutionary biology and primatology, to make his point, but the upshot is clear: we continue to march on toward the end of history, with just a thirty-five-year cultural disruption to slow us down.

What should we think of Fukuyama on democratic capitalism's recent history? *The Great Disruption* contains a wealth of data that will be mined for years to come. But Fukuyama's argument is in some ways as overstated as Gray's.

To begin with, his explanation of the Great Disruption is unsatisfactory. There is a stronger cultural component—an autonomous component—to moral breakdown in the West than Fukuyama concedes. If the transition from an industrial to a postindustrial economy undermined moral life throughout the Western democracies, why didn't the same change lead to disorder in Japan and South Korea? As Fukuyama admits, nothing comparable to the divorce and illegitimacy of the West exists in these Asian societies. Crime rates in Japan actually dropped during the period of the Great Disruption. Apparently, the "thicker" communal and familial cultures of Asian societies staved off disorder. But this would indicate, against the main thrust of Fukuyama's argument, that culture moves independently from economics. Moreover, the Pill didn't drop out of the sky one day on unsuspecting liberal societies, but was the consequence of profound cultural and moral movements—particularly the rise of feminism—that thus far have had less resonance in Asia.

Nor does Fukuyama sufficiently stress the role of law and policy in the West's social woes. Would divorce have increased so dramatically had Western societies not liberalized divorce laws? Would crime have so ravaged America's cities in the absence of laws coddling criminals? Would the number of abortions have skyrocketed had liberal regimes not legalized abortion? No. The postindustrial economy didn't force these changes in law and policy. Rather, they too reflected profound cultural and moral shifts—especially the triumph in elite circles of liberal attitudes—that thus far haven't penetrated Asian societies to the same degree. In short, culture and politics seem to be the primary explanatory factors for the Great Disruption, not capitalist economics.

Culture and politics are the principal realms of man's liberty and reason. Fukuyama's refusal to grant them a major place in his analysis follows from his reductive conception of human nature, which, despite his claims, is anything but Aristotelian. The methods of the behavioral sciences from which he draws are rigidly deterministic. Fukuyama protests that he is no determinist. But I wonder if it is possible to embrace these sciences uncritically, as he does, and still leave a place for freedom. Evolutionary biology, for example, with its theory of the "selfish gene," interprets a mother's sacrifice for her child not as a free act of love but as a quest to propagate her genetic heritage. This interpretation is untestable. Yet if it's a matter of belief, why believe it? Doing so, as Berlin wrote of similar deterministic theories decades ago, renders our moral vocabulary vacant and the human world literally senseless. If his notion of freedom is thin, Fukuyama's understanding of human reason isn't much thicker. It teaches us the most efficient way to get from A to B, and that's about it.

Given Fukuyama's reliance on untenable economic and scientific reductionisms, his optimism about moral renewal in liberal democratic societies inspires only so much confidence. Man's nature limits his freedom, but within those limits experiments in living can take him far from recognizably good ways of life, where his faculties can thrive, toward ways of life that diminish his spirit and lead, in the long run, to social breakdown. Who can say how long a society can continue to exist—much less improve—while its spiritual life declines? Furthermore, why should we expect the same postindustrial economy Fukuyama thinks led to the Great Disruption automatically to heal it? Simply because an economy "needs" something doesn't mean human beings will supply it.

Radicalizing Moral Libertinism

Yet both Gray and Fukuyama do brush up against the truth. When moral nihilism dominates a culture, free markets can radicalize that nihilism by shouting it, so to speak, from the rooftops. A serious threat to the future of democratic capitalism, I believe, lies in the association of capitalist power and moral libertinism. A few years ago, Buttiglione made a pregnant observation: "Libertinism is in a certain sense more dangerous than Marxism, because it penetrates more deeply." Instead of crushing man's reason and his passions, as did communism, moral libertinism turns man's passions against the truth. Marxism, as we've seen, was a religious atheism, a secular religion that proposed to build utopia only to open the gates of hell. Libertinism, Buttiglione maintains, is a "negative atheism"—it "corrupts societies and is unable to offer the values needed for a society to live." Not everyone can, as a matter of moral philosophy, "just do it," or else society crumbles. In the long run, Buttiglione thinks libertine capitalism "is existentially unbearable." But in the short run—and that can last a long time—it can do immense damage.

Gray and Fukuyama are right, then, to see a link between contemporary capitalism and nihilism, but they get things backward. Nihilism is first *imported into* the market, not exported from it. Nihilism results, Buttiglione says, from the "suicide of culture," and here he means culture in the sense of *Bildung*, or soul-formation, not as an anthropological term. Our elite spiritual enterprises too rarely seek the true, the good, and the beautiful, however plural and difficult to attain these ends might be. The suicide of culture sends its tenebrous signals throughout the human world; the market often receives these signals, dumbs them down or brightens them up, and then seduces whomever it can.

The connection between nihilism and capitalism is accidental. The struggle against the former requires not a refusal to reconcile ourselves to this-worldly realities, such as democratic capitalism's politics and economics, but rather something much more inspired: the renewal of culture. That is where we should direct our spiritual longings. Politics, too, can play its part. Statesmanship can help set society's moral and aesthetic tone, and postliberal policies, like those New York City has successfully implemented in fighting crime and reforming welfare, can chip away at the decisions that fed the Great Disruption.

Here is what the democratic capitalist prospect looks like during the first decade of the new millennium: in politics, it finds itself haunted by moral indeterminacy and weak before egalitarian demands; in economics, troubled by the anxieties of the rapid change that creates wealth; and in culture, suffering from confusion in the elevated pursuits that should protect man's highest ends. Not pretty, until you realize the alternatives—some new nightmare arising from bourgeois discontents, a spirit-sapping tutelary despotism, or a radicalization of libertine nihilism.

Working a slight change on an old truism: democratic capitalism is still the worst regime, except for all the others. Perhaps, if we're both vigilant and lucky, the twenty-first century will not rival Berlin's twentieth as "the most terrible in Western history."

2

The Ineducable Left

The far Left's disgraceful response to September 11–it has temporized about terror, proposed as morally equivalent the actions of those Islamist fanatics who killed thousands of innocent Americans and the military response of a democratically elected government, and even blamed the United States for the atrocity–shows that its hatred of democratic capitalism and, more broadly, Western civilization itself remains fierce more than a decade after the collapse of socialism. The intensity of this antagonism will come as no surprise, however, to anyone who has paid attention to the praise that the academic Left and its sympathizers in the liberal media have showered on one of the most pernicious books published in recent memory: Michael Hardt and Antonio Negri's encomium to anticapitalist revolutionary violence, *Empire*.

This forbidding five-hundred-page book of political and social theory, which ends with a surreal celebration of "the irrepressible lightness and joy of being communist," is that rare commodity: a genuine academic bestseller. Its publisher, Harvard University Press, has put the book through multiple printings and has sold foreign translation rights to publishers in at least ten other nations across the globe. For a good while after its 2001 release, upscale bookstores had a hard time keeping the volume in stock. *Empire* has become a key reference in academic critical theory courses.

Small wonder, given the eye-popping reviews it has received. Postmodernism guru Frederic Jameson calls it "prophetic" and "the first great new theoretical synthesis of the new millennium." Slavonian philosopher Slavoj Zizek celebrates it as "nothing less than a rewriting of *The Communist Manifesto* for our time" (this, needless to say, he deems a good thing). "Brilliant," "erudite," "extraordinary," "an amazing tour de force," "irresistible," "revolutionary," "a work of visionary intensity"—left-wing intellectuals have exhausted superlatives describing it. The liberal press has been just as enthusiastic. The *New York Times*, in a glowing write-up, crowned *Empire* the "Next Big Idea." *Time* breathlessly commended it as "the hot, smart book of the moment." The influential British weekly the *New Statesman* gushed that *Empire* had "turned conventional thinking on its head." Not since Michel Foucault's history of sexuality started appearing in English translation two decades ago has a work of high theory produced such palpitations on the left.

What's all the excitement about? In part, it is the book's grandiose ambition that generated the buzz. Hardt and Negri seek to update Marx's *Capital* for the era of economic globalization. In doing so, they plunder every imaginable recent source of academic foolishness, from postcolonialism to queer theory to French poststructuralism, and wed it to Marx, Lenin, and even Mao, making the book a kind of up-to-the-minute manual on how to get tenure in today's university. *Empire*'s pages brim with the science-fiction-like neologisms that typify much contemporary academic writing: "agentic," "biopower," "deterritorialization"—words that give those who wield them the sense of having shaman-like access to hidden realms. And unlike most leftist writing since the fall of communism, which has been dourly pessimistic, *Empire* is also brash and optimistic, heralding the revolutionary dawn of a utopian postcapitalist age.

The Terrorist Philosopher

But the deeper reason for the book's popularity, I think, is the unusual biography of *Empire*'s Italian coauthor Antonio Negri. The book's jacket matter-of-factly informs us that he is "an independent researcher and writer" before getting around to mentioning that he's also an "inmate at Rebibbia Prison, Rome." You see, in addition to his career as an influential political philosopher, with widely translated books on Spinoza and Marx to his credit, Negri is a convicted terrorist.

In 1979, the Italian government arrested Negri, at the time a political science professor at the University of Padua, and accused him of being the secret brains behind the Red Brigades, the Italian version of the Weathermen in the United States or the Baader-Meinhoff Gang in West Germany—left-wing groups that during the 1970s sought to overthrow capitalist regimes through campaigns of terrorist violence. Italian authorities believed that Negri himself had planned the infamous 1979 kidnapping and murder of Aldo Moro, the leader of Italy's Christian Democratic Party. Just before Moro's execution, his distraught wife got a taunting phone call, telling her that her husband was about to die. The voice was allegedly Negri's. Unable to build a strong enough case to try the philosopher for murder, Italian authorities convicted him on the lesser charge of "armed insurrection against the state."

Negri's theoretical work was in keeping with his terrorist activities. He had become the leading voice of Italy's ultra-left by advancing an inventive reinterpretation of Marx's *Grundrisse* that located the agent of social revolution not among the industrial proletariat, largely co-opted as it was by capitalist wealth and bourgeois democratic freedoms, but among those marginalized from economic and political life: criminals, part-time workers, the unemployed. Negri believed that these dispossessed souls would be far quicker to unleash the riotous confrontations with the state that he thought necessary for destroying capitalism.

After much legal wrangling, and facing thirty years in prison, Negri eventually fled to France, where during the mid-eighties he became chums with philosopher Gilles Deleuze and other radical thinkers, lectured at the University of Paris (where he met the student who would become his American coauthor, Duke literature professor Michael Hardt), and wrote a host of books and essays, including paeans to the "politics of subversion" and a bizarre meditation on St. Francis of Assisi as a proto-communist.

Then, a few years ago, after nearly two decades in exile, an unrepentant Negri returned to Italy to serve a reduced sentence. The book-jacket claim that he was an inmate at Ribibbia was exaggerated. In fact, Negri, released in the spring of 2003, was serving his time under partial house arrest at his book-lined apartment in a tony Rome neighborhood. He had to sleep there at night, but was otherwise free to come and go as he pleased, and he regularly received fawning journalists and academics seeking the master's wisdom.

Negri's criminal past grants *Empire* a veneer of revolutionary authenticity and gives readers predisposed to feel it that agreeable frisson which results from transgressing bourgeois conventions. As writer David Pryce-Jones observes, Negri "brings with him the glamour of murder." Few things, he notes, are more alluring to the armchair radicals of academe and the *New York Times*.

Evil Empire

What is the argument, such as it is, of this strange book? For Hardt and Negri, "Empire" is "the sovereign power that governs the world"—a new "capitalist mode of production." It is, more concretely, the global market. At the pinnacle of Empire is the capitalist power par excellence, the nuclear-bomb-wielding United States, "a superpower that can act alone but prefers to act in collaboration with others." Among those others: the G-8 nations, the Paris and London Clubs for Growth, and various nongovernmental organizations that seek to expand economic exchanges among states. The vertiginous market forces that these political and economic bodies have unleashed are destroying the old imperialistic nation-state and creating in its stead a new transpolitical global order where economic considerations trump all other concerns. "In its ideal form," the authors write, "there is no outside to the world market: the entire globe is its domain." Quoting Polybius, Hardt and Negri draw an explicit parallel between the new Empire's continent-spanning reach and Rome's mastery of the Mediterranean world in antiquity.

Economic globalization, Hardt and Negri assert in Marxoid language, has meant that a handful of rich folks are getting richer and more powerful at the expense of the vast majority, who grow "always more exploited," more abject, more "proletarianized." The new global order claims to promote peace, they charge, but in practice it is "bathed in blood." Any time Empire senses a danger to the circulation of commodities, whether Islamic "terrorists" (the scare quotes are Hardt and Negri's) or Mexican revolutionaries, out come the guns and missiles to deal with the threat. Today's Empire, like its Roman predecessor, is a brutal pacifying force.

What makes Empire truly insidious, though, is that people internalize the ways of life it promotes. Citizens of prosperous liberal democracies only seem to be free. In reality, say Hardt and Negri, they are subjects of terrifying "societies of control," consumed in the "rhythm of productive practices and productive socialization." Capitalism, in short, creates capitalist men and women, automatons buying what the market says to buy and dutifully trudging to work in the "social factory." "The great industrial and financial powers," the authors warn, "produce not only commodities but also subjectivities," or individuals whose very "needs, social relations, bodies, and minds" respond mechanically to the market's call.

Yet all is not lost. Hardt and Negri hold that, even as Empire seduces, it sows the seeds of its possible destruction. Gestating within the womb of economic globalization is a "counter-Empire," led by "the multitude"—the authors' stand-in for Marx's proletariat (and the title of *Empire*'s less successful 2004 sequel). The multitude includes all those men and women who don't fit neatly into the global capitalist economy. Have-nots across the planet, the antiglobalization movement, Latin revolutionaries, inner-city blacks, drug addicts, anti-family women, drag queens, body piercers, Islamic radicals, and anyone else who rejects bourgeois values—together these constitute the nomadic "against-men" of the multitude. Just as the Christians of the late Roman Empire colonized its spiritual universe from within, so the against-men will overcome the new Empire. The political task of the third millennium, the authors believe—they stress that they are not vulgar historical determinists, so political action is essential—will be to help bring this multitude together so that it can forge "an alternative political organization of global flows and exchanges" that "will one day take us through and beyond Empire."

What will this "alternative political organization" look like? Hardt and Negri, like their intellectual godfather Marx, remain mostly silent about the postcapitalist world, but they do offer a few provocative hints. Global citizenship will be one key feature. "The cities of the earth will become at once great deposits of cooperating humanity and locomotives for circulation, temporary residences and networks of the mass distribution of living humanity—an end to borders and nations," they prophesy. A second aspect will be "absolute democracy," in which the multitude directly manages and organizes economic, political, and social life. No more will private property—"a putrid and tyrannical obsolescence"—pit man against man. Free access to and control over "knowledge, information, communication, and affects" will be a matter of course. A final characteristic: equal compensation for all. Hardt and Negri call it a "citizenship income."

The counter-Empire will become possible only after modernity—including the universal solvent of global capitalism—has dissolved the certainties of earlier ages. Hardt and Negri's multitude is a colossal power, born with the modern age's emancipation of the human will from the moral constraints of religion and human nature. "Today there is not even the illusion of a transcendent God," the authors proclaim. "The mythology of the languages of the multitude interprets the telos of the earthly city, torn away by the power of its own destiny from any belonging or subjection to a city of God, which has lost all honor and legitimacy." Human nature is a mirage, too. We must embrace our "posthuman" identities as monkeys and cyborgs. "Humanism after the death of Man," the authors call their stark vision of man as demiurge. The multitude represents an "uncontainable force," an "excess of value with respect to every form of right and law." Beyond good and evil, it will "create and recreate" the human world in a "secular Pentecost." Dreaming of communist supermen, Hardt and Negri view the American Declaration of Independence and the Marx-inspired revolutions of the twentieth century as anticipatory signs of the coming liberation.

These epochal transformations will require a cleansing bloodletting. "The new barbarians" of the multitude must "destroy with an affirmative violence and trace new paths of life through their own material existence." Hardt and Negri's language bristles at the multitude's bourgeois enemies:

> Who wants to see any more of that pallid and parasitic European ruling class that led directly from the ancien régime to nationalism, from populism to fascism, and now pushes for a generalized neoliberalism? Who wants to see more of those ideologies and those bureaucratic apparatuses that have nourished and abetted the rotting European elites? And who can still stand those systems of labor organization and those corporations that have stripped away every vital spirit?

Inhumanism

The success of *Empire* is astonishing when you cut through the jargon and consider exactly what it says. Hardt and Negri fall prey to every destructive error that has characterized radical antibourgeois thought, of the Left and Right, from Lenin to Heidegger to Foucault to Islamism. Though the book seems on first inspection to be offering something new, it is really very old news.

Like their radical predecessors, Hardt and Negri fail to think politically—fail to explore the real possibilities and dangers of political reality and take measure of the lessons of history. Though the authors say they want to mine the "dense complex of experience"—a praiseworthy aim for any kind of political thinking—the reader of *Empire* will wander through hundreds of pages of theory before he encounters a flesh-and-blood political actor, or a real decision, or a historical event, or an existing institution. The book, like much contemporary political theory, is inhumanly abstract. The same abstraction was abundantly evident when Hardt appeared on *The Charlie Rose Show.* To the host's commonsense questions, Hardt could only respond in hallucinatory theory-speak. To anyone unfamiliar with the latest academic buzzwords, he sounded like a space alien. Rose seemed—justifiably—completely befuddled.

Since they fail to think politically, it is no surprise that Hardt and Negri also offer no evidence to support their basic charge that economic globalization is causing planetary misery. Predictably, as the 2001 G-8 meeting got underway in Genoa, Italy, the *New York Times* chose these two "joyful" communists to write a lengthy op-ed extolling the virtues of antiglobalization rioters.

The truth about globalization is exactly the reverse of what Hardt and Negri assert. Globalization is dramatically increasing world prosperity and freedom. As the *Economist*'s John Micklethwait and Adrian Wooldridge point out, in the half century since the foundation of the General Agreement on Tariffs and Trade (GATT), the world economy has expanded six-fold, in part because trade has increased 1,600 percent; nations open to trade grow nearly twice as fast as those that aren't; and World Bank data show that during the last decade of the twentieth century—a time of accelerated economic globalization—approximately 800 million people escaped poverty.

Needless to say, economic globalization isn't without its downside. As I've argued in chapter 1, it can—there's no necessity at work—amplify and disseminate some of the less elevated aspects of today's Western culture. But on balance, the empirical evidence proves it far preferable to any alternative economic order we know of. It has profoundly diminished human suffering.

If Hardt and Negri's depiction of global capitalism is mendacious, their hazy alternative to it—absolute democracy, open borders, equal compensation—is apolitical utopian nonsense. How would such schemes actually work? Hardt and Negri never say. Do they truly think that "annulling" private property and eliminating nations, if it were somehow possible, would be liberating? Wouldn't it lead to a totalitarian increase in political power, as in the old Soviet Union? But then Hardt and Negri seem to look back fondly on Lenin and Stalin's dark regime. "Cold war ideology called that society totalitarian," they complain, "but in fact it was a society criss-crossed by extremely strong instances of creativity and freedom, just as strong as the rhythms of economic development and cultural modernization." To which one can only respond: Have they never read a page of Solzhenitsyn? Moreover, as filled with admiration as Hardt and Negri are toward the Soviet Union, they are contemptuous toward the decencies and the humble—and often not so humble—freedoms of democratic capitalist societies.

Along with this failure to look at political reality, Hardt and Negri share another characteristic with Lenin, Franz Fanon, and many other antibourgeois thinkers: a totalitarian style of thought that substitutes rhetorical violence for reasoned argument. For Lenin, disagreement with the revolutionary line (as he defined it) was heretical. Differences of political vision and even pragmatic disputes were not open to moderation through debate, as in the liberal democratic tradition, but deserved only insult—and, in practice, ruthless elimination. Hardt and Negri's violent verbal attacks on Western capitalists—"putrid," "rotting," "parasitic"—could have been lifted right from the pages of Lenin's *Materialism and Empirio-criticism* (or, for that matter, from one of Osama bin Laden's manifestos). After September 11, the authors' illiberal, terrorist language seems obscene.

Hardt and Negri's contempt for the bourgeois men and women who go to work, attend church, raise their kids, and generally live respectable, productive lives is itself contemptible. Who do these two men think they are? How did they free themselves from the "society of control" while most of us fritter away our lives as drones in the social factory? *Empire*'s elitism is an updated version of the Marxian notion of a revolutionary vanguard, another terrible idea that helped spawn the political evils of the last century.

Hardt and Negri's final delusion is their cartoon version of the modern world as completely secularized. Tell that to the Islamist fanatics who made bombs out of planes, praying to Allah as they died, or to the friends and relatives of those they killed who crowded into churches and synagogues seeking meaning and solace for their suffering. For both good and ill, as André Malraux predicted, the twenty-first century clearly will be religious, not secular. Hardt and Negri believe that something decent will arise from their lawless atheism. But why assume justice will prevail from such nihilism, when everything we know from history—the wounded history of the twentieth century above all—says that it results invariably in the law of the jungle? Without morality and the rule of law, the powerful simply feel free to rape and pillage; the weak can only tremble and hide.

Apolitical abstraction and wild-eyed utopianism, a terroristic approach to political argument, hatred for flesh-and-blood human beings, nihilism: *Empire* is a poisonous brew of bad ideas. It belongs in the library of political madness.

Do Hardt and Negri's many fans really believe their own praise? Does *Time* really think it's "smart" to call for the eradication of private property, celebrate revolutionary violence, whitewash totalitarianism, and pour contempt on the genuine achievements of liberal democracies and capitalist economics? Would Frederic Jameson like to give up his big salary at Duke? To ask such questions is to answer them. The far Left gets its kicks in the adolescent thrill of perpetual rebellion. Too many of those who should know better refuse to grow up. The ghost of Marx haunts us still.

II. The American Difference

3

From State to Civil Society

The last century witnessed an extraordinary growth in government power, a result of the faith millions placed in the state as an agent of the human will and as the instrument of political and economic emancipation. In its most extreme forms, driven by the secular religions of National Socialism and communism, the newly empowered state caused incalculable human suffering. But even in the decent welfare democracies of the West, it fell far short of the hopes placed in it.

In America, the activist liberal welfare state–growing out of the Progressive movement of the early twentieth century, given institutional form in Franklin D. Roosevelt's New Deal, and vastly expanded in the Great Society and the War on Poverty launched by Lyndon B. Johnson in the mid-sixties– had a noble goal: to eradicate poverty, especially among the nation's disadvantaged blacks. The assumption behind welfare was that poverty was only a material condition. Temporarily give people the food, money, and shelter they needed to better their lives, and they would soon become responsible and independent.

Tragically, it didn't work out that way. Despite the trillions spent on government poverty programs since the sixties–during a time, it is important to add, of growing opportunity, when millions of immigrants, most of them poor, flooded into the country and found success through hard work and short-term sacrifice—the numbers of the poor have not declined. And in some ways their condition actually worsened. For millions, especially those concentrated in mostly minority inner-city neighborhoods, welfare became a dysfunctional, intergenerational way of life, associated with an array of social pathologies, including an atrophied sense of personal responsibility, rampant illegitimacy, and high levels of substance abuse, school failure, and crime. Welfare programs, losing sight of their clients' real needs, became ends in themselves, with bureaucratic constituencies fiercely resisting reform and a class of politicians willing to protect and benefit from them.

Recognizing the failure of statist liberal nostrums to help the worst off, many social thinkers and policy experts in recent years have been attracted by the idea of encouraging civil society—those value-transmitting "mediating institutions" such as the family, churches, and voluntary associations which stand between the individual and the state—to assume chief responsibility for assisting the down-and-out. This "civil society project," as some term it, is one of the most significant intellectual and practical developments of our age. Its influence is particularly powerful in America, less so in Europe's social democracies. It lies behind the 1996 welfare reform act that ended the federal entitlement to welfare, and it infuses President George W. Bush's initiative to turn to private faith-based institutions to aid the needy (though some critics see the Bush administration's penchant for government activism as letting down the civil society cause). If the twentieth century was the era of the state, the twenty-first may be the era of civil society.

What Is Government's Proper Role in Social Relief?

In hindsight, welfare's failure to help society's have-nots reflected a fundamental misunderstanding of government's proper role. In his 1991 social encyclical *Centesimus Annus,* Pope John Paul II severely criticized the "excesses and abuses" of the welfare state—or the "social assistance state," in his words. The welfare state robbed society of its responsibilities, the encyclical argued, leading to a "loss of human energies and an inordinate increase of public agencies, which are dominated more by bureaucratic ways of thinking than by concern for serving their clients, and which are accompanied by an enormous increase in spending." These problems flow from the welfare state's violation of the classic Catholic principle of subsidiarity, which holds that a "community of a higher order should not interfere in the internal life of a community of a lower order, depriving the latter of its functions, but rather should support it in case of need and help coordinate its activity with the rest of society, always with a view to the common good." In assisting the needy, subsidiarity holds that responsibility should rest first with the individual, and then, in ascending order, with those nearest to him: family, friends, neighborhood, church, voluntary institutions, local government, and finally—only as a last resort—the state.

The reason for this preference for the local is simple: "Needs are best understood and satisfied by people who are closest to them and who act as neighbors to those in need." Helping a junkie kick a crack habit or teaching an inner-city teen the social skills necessary to hold down a job or showing a young single mother that a life on the dole isn't the best she can do, for herself or for her kids—these kinds of crucial *moral* tasks call for a better response than simply handing out government benefits, no questions asked, which was the reigning spirit of public assistance until at least the mid-nineties. Rather, they call for the presence of someone "capable of perceiving the deeper human need." Government welfare programs, which by law must treat similarly situated individuals alike, have a nearly impossible task in differentiating the endlessly various needs of recipients, whom they have tended to treat as mere objects.

There is no more telling example of the dangers of disregarding subsidiarity than the fact that welfare has tended to replace fathers in poor urban communities. In inner-city neighborhoods, where at its height welfare became a regular part of everyday life, illegitimacy rates rocketed to 80 percent. Whole generations of kids have grown up not only without fathers (except in the crude biological sense), but also without knowing anybody with a real father. Welfare hasn't been the only factor driving up illegitimacy, of course. A bigger reason, perhaps, has been the moral transvaluation that took root in the sixties, which so eroded constraints on sexual behavior that having a child outside of marriage eventually carried little stigma among the urban poor, or among anyone else (on this, see Myron Magnet's classic work of social history *The Dream and the Nightmare*). But welfare certainly did its part by easing the immediate financial costs of illegitimacy. Instead of marrying the fathers of their children, many young women began to "marry" the state. The consequences, as all but the most blinkered ideologues now recognize, have been devastating. Children born out of wedlock have a far higher rate of social failure along an array of indicators—from levels of economic success and educational achievement to rates of criminality, drug abuse, and suicide—than those who grow up in intact, two-parent families. Illegitimacy remains a serious American problem.

In a related way, welfare corroded the personal responsibility essential to a self-governing society. By severing the connection between getting help and giving something back (like work), the "entitlement" to public assistance depressed "human energies," just as Tocqueville predicted over 150 years ago. In his prescient *Memoir on Pauperism*, Tocqueville wrestled with a paradox: Why was it that the poorest countries of Europe had few able-bodied indigent, while prosperous England had many? The answer, Tocqueville believed, was England's system of public charity, which, for some, undermined any motive to work. Getting by was enough if one could do so without sweating for supper. Instead of reducing pauperism, in other words, the dole made it more prevalent. Tocqueville didn't think that complex modern industrial societies could avoid systems of public welfare. But they would come with this corrupting cost.

Thus, the spiritual torpor that characterized America's welfare system (a mutation in social psychology just like the one Tocqueville described) occurred almost simultaneously with the 1965 launch of the War on Poverty. Even though the national economy was booming (unemployment had hit record lows), the welfare rolls began rapidly to swell as President Johnson's reforms both increased welfare benefits and made it easier to get them. The welfare trap had sprung. Already in 1971, social critic Irving Kristol could write: "The number of eligible poor who actually apply for welfare will increase as welfare benefits go up—as they did throughout the 1960s. When welfare payments (and associated benefits, such as Medicaid and food stamps) compete with low wages, many poor people will rationally prefer welfare."

Revealingly, and as Tocqueville would have predicted, the introduction of time limits on welfare has led many long-term recipients to leave the welfare rolls and seek work.

Civil Society: The Itinerary of an Idea

The turn to civil society in recent reflection and policy has sought to ameliorate the problem of entrenched poverty in ways much more in keeping with the principle of subsidiarity than has been true of the liberal welfare state.

"Civil society" has meant several different things in the history of social philosophy. Increasingly present as a concept in political thought from the mid-eighteenth century on, two broad—and somewhat antithetical—interpretations eventually took shape. The first, Hegelian and Marxist in inspiration, saw civil society as the realm of economic and class contradictions ("the battlefield where everyone's individual private interest meets everyone else's," as Hegel described it) that were distinct from the state but required resolution through state action. The second, born with the Anglo-Scottish Enlightenment and thinkers like Adam Ferguson, David Hume, and Adam Smith, saw civil society as a self-regulating realm (again, apart from the state) that required protection from government control. It's this second tradition that has resonated in the American context. "Civil society is composed of all those associations, freely chosen or natural (such as the family), through which citizens practice self-government independent of the state," observes Michael Novak. "Through the institutions of civil society and its mediating structures, citizens pursue their own affairs, accomplish their social purposes, and enrich the texture of their common life. Civil society is a larger, more basic, and more vital component of social life and the common good than the state is. The state is the servant of civil society. This is caught in Lincoln's classic phrase: 'government of the people, by the people, and for the people.'"

Religious congregations, civic groups, business firms and associations, labor unions, homeschooling networks, Little

League, self-help societies, the proliferating interconnected groups of the Web—in the United States, civil society swarms with citizens pursuing an almost limitless number and variety of goals. This knack for association struck Tocqueville as a major difference between America and France. "Americans of all ages, all conditions, all minds unite," he wrote in *Democracy in America.*

> Not only do they have commercial and industrial associations in which all take part, but they also have a thousand other kinds: religious, moral, grave, futile, very general and very particular, immense and very small. . . . Everywhere that, at the head of a new undertaking, you see the government in France and a great lord in England, count on it that you will perceive an association in the United States.

How Can Civil Society Uplift the Poor?

The civil society project is thus in keeping with a profoundly American characteristic. But how can civil society help the poor? Historian Gertrude Himmelfarb parses the argument: It is in the families and communities of civil society that the moral life blossoms and people learn about duties and personal responsibility, not just rights and self-interest. Civil society has the moral resources to understand "the deeper human need" of the poor.

Civil society's key institution in this light is the family, and for two reasons. First, it is primarily in the family that we become self-governing citizens. As children we have our characters—our habits of mind and will and our basic values—molded there, and our life courses, if not predetermined, are thereby at least profoundly influenced. Human children, very different in this regard from other animals, require a long period of educational, emotional, and spiritual nurturing before reaching adulthood, and this takes place primarily in the family. The family also serves as a kind of economic enterprise, building up wealth and contacts over time. How many of us got first jobs through family contacts, washing dishes in an uncle's friend's greasy spoon, say, or cutting lawns for an older cousin's landscaping firm? How many young families get financial help from both the husband's and the wife's families in buying a first home, or even in the form of free babysitting?

In both functions—nurturing well-rounded, self-governing adults and serving as a community of mutual support—the traditional two-parent family has vast advantages over single-parent, female-headed families (and, needless to say, over government programs). All things being equal, two parents bring not only their own moral and financial capital to bear on rearing children, but that of both extended families. A single parent usually can't compete.

A thriving neighborhood can help struggling individuals and families, too. A neighborhood where civil society has wilted, where, as in many American inner cities still, a condition of near-Hobbesian aggression prevails, can suffocate the human spirit. Conversely, a successful community, like a healthy family, encourages it to prosper. Friends and neighbors will typically watch out, for instance, to make sure that one's child doesn't fall in with the wrong crowd. Or they might babysit the kids during the day so a parent can work. Neighbors can also be wonderful sources of advice, shopping tips, childrearing know-how, and innumerable other forms of social knowledge.

Furthermore, the voluntary associations of civil society can (and do) uplift the needy. Churches stand at the front lines of this effort. After all, if a major part of reducing poverty is to alter dysfunctional lives, what does the job more effectively than robust religion? Traditional religion–the kind espoused by Catholic charities until the 1960s, for example– stresses personal responsibility to self and family, prescribes an authoritative set of rights and wrongs, provides a sense of community, and promises forgiveness for past mistakes if one makes a new start. Nonreligious associations often do this, too. Created over one hundred years ago as a response to the moral and physical problems of impoverished inner-city youth, the Boy Scouts inculcate not just a body of technical knowledge but also a set of vital character-building virtues– including self-reliance, hard work, and honesty–that today's inner-city youth desperately need. As my Manhattan Institute colleague Heather Mac Donald has chronicled, the Boy Scouts still do exemplary work among the urban poor, doing more to alleviate poverty than any number of cumbersome government poverty programs.

Private charities (often religiously motivated) are indispensable voluntary institutions in combating poverty. Americans are an immensely generous people, giving more than $200 billion to charities in 2005. More than two-thirds of all Americans donate to tax-exempt organizations every year. If you combine volunteer work–about half of all Americans dedicate some of their time to philanthropic activities–the worth of charitable efforts scales well over $300 billion.

Private charities have significant advantages over government poverty programs. Unlike government programs, they don't have to treat everybody alike. Cato Institute policy expert Michael Tanner explains how this can make a huge difference. "Take, for example, the case of a poor person who has a job offer. But she can't get to the job because her car battery is dead," he says. "A government welfare program can do nothing but tell her to wait two weeks until her welfare check arrives. Of course, by that time the job will be gone. A private charity can simply go out and buy a car battery (or even jump-start the dead battery)."

A privately run drug rehabilitation clinic, to take another example, can vary its approach to each of its clients as it sees fit. Some might need intensive oversight, lots of time, and tough love. Others might be more self-motivated and need a lighter touch. Government programs can't be so flexible. Nor do private charities waste as much money on bureaucratic overhead. In government poverty programs, nearly two-thirds of the money earmarked for the poor winds up in the pockets of social workers and bureaucrats. In addition, private "faith-based" charities don't have to water down their religious identities, whereas government regulations have prevented religious charities with government contracts from including a strong religious message with their services, which makes those services less effective.

Finally, private charity reestablishes the moral reciprocity between donor and giver that government entitlements abrogate. Consider the St. Martin de Porres House of Hope, a shelter for homeless women, many of them drug addicts and unmarried with kids, located in Chicago's blighted Woodlawn neighborhood. Over the years, the charity has stayed away from government money so that it can operate with no strings attached. It requires any young woman who comes looking for help immediately to start working around the house, sending a clear message of responsibility. Clients' days overflow with activity—self-help meetings, GED classes, instruction in responsible sexual behavior, and lots more—focused on building up what social theorists call human capital. But if the House of Hope's charges don't follow the rules, they're back on the streets. The charity wields both stick and carrot. More importantly, it gets results. Reportedly, only 5 percent of the women who complete its program return to homeless shelters.

Another actor in civil society that helps the poor is business. Many thinkers don't include businesses (at least big corporations) in civil society. But in fact, businesses are essential civil-society agents: "they support research, the arts, charities, and good works of many kinds, and they undergird the financial hopes of American families," Novak writes. "Above all, they expand the space for independence and private action in the public sphere."

Businesses can help the poor both directly and indirectly. One obvious direct way is by creating jobs. It's a far better thing to generate enough jobs for everyone willing to work than to make people dependent on government handouts. Even for the most dysfunctional, this is often true. In reaching out to the worst off, for example, many firms have become involved with both public and private welfare-to-work initiatives by hiring former welfare recipients in various entry-level positions. These jobs provide welfare clients with valuable work experience and teach them essential work-related habits like showing up on time, being civil to coworkers and customers, and dressing appropriately.

Firms also help society's have-nots by giving to charity and by encouraging employees to be upstanding citizens in the local community. Businesses aren't welfare organizations, of course. Their first responsibilities are to customers, workers, and shareholders. But they have a strong stake in promoting self-government and a responsible citizenry. After all, absent these things, government swells, pushing up taxes that cut into profits in order to pay for its expanding size. Indirectly, firms aid the needy by creating low-cost products. From "generic" product brands to used cars, a productive free-market economy is endlessly inventive in making life easier for those lacking resources.

A Post–Welfare State Agenda

Although in a post-welfare society it would no longer be the primary, direct source of aid to the poor, government could still do many things to bolster civil society's antipoverty efforts. (I follow here Novak's imaginative discussion in his *Catholic Ethic and the Spirit of Capitalism.*)

For instance, government could use its bully pulpit to direct the public's attention to needed tasks. Or it could craft laws that help citizens become self-governing—that boost work, savings, ownership, savings, and personal accountability. A third activity: to design incentives for firms and individuals to contribute to charities, or, more controversially, directly to fund religious charities for the pursuit of public purposes (as President Bush's Office of Faith-Based and Community Initiatives has tried to do). A fourth would be to establish greater educational choice, giving the poor new private-sector educational options instead of forcing them to remain in lousy public schools. And finally, a fifth role of government could be to continue to implement those successful urban crime-fighting methods adopted in the 1990s which have helped the tendrils of civil society to shoot forth again in formerly blighted, crime-ridden, inner-city neighborhoods.

Turning to civil society obviously won't solve all of our social problems. Every arrangement of social institutions gives rise to unintended consequences that future generations will have to seek imperfectly to improve. Moreover, some institutions of civil society have succumbed to the same cultural forces that made the welfare state so counterproductive by promoting ideas antagonistic to the kind of moral character civil society should build. Many large foundations and charities, for example, practice a firm nonjudgmentalism, taking the view that the primary problems of the poor are material rather than behavioral. Solving those problems, say these philanthropies, merely requires the transfer of more material goods. In some cases, private charitable institutions have themselves become grossly dependent on government funds. And many businesses promote antibourgeois values through their products and charitable giving. When civil society gets corrupted in this fashion, it betrays its promise.

But after fifty years of failed government efforts to defeat poverty, the civil society project is the best chance we have to reduce the numbers of the long-term poor and build a democratic capitalism that better promotes human dignity.

4

Religious America, Secular Europe

A merica and Europe, or at least the nations of "old" west-ern Europe, have been increasingly at odds since the end of the Cold War. Even a casual observer can see this in the rampant anti-Americanism prevalent on the Continent. The hostility manifests itself with particular force among elites: The European Union deputy and French political scientist Olivier Duhamel, to take just one example, describes the United States as a "degenerate" democracy—an irrational na-tion and a threat to global order. A 2003 international poll ranked the American "hyperpower" second only to Israel as the greatest danger to world peace. Political relations be-tween the United States and Europe have become so chilly that France and Germany openly worked to undermine their long-time ally in the run-up to war in Iraq.

One should not overstate the importance of these ten-sions within the democratic world. Nobody is predicting that Belgium and the United States will be firing missiles at each other any time soon, or ever. But as Robert Kagan has observed, it sometimes seems nowadays as if Americans and Europeans live on different planets. A variety of expla-nations has been offered for the widening rift, among them the end of the Cold War, which has deprived the Western democracies of a powerful common enemy against which to unify; contrasting views of the comparative importance of national sovereignty and international institutions; use of the death penalty in the United States; and anger over the Bush administration's decision to use military force to prosecute the global struggle against Islamist terror. One of the most significant sources of tension and lack of mutual understanding between America and Europe, however, is religion—or better, America's religiosity, and Europe's practical agnosticism.

A Post-Christian Europe

Europe is becoming a very secular place. As the general secretary of the United Reform Church in Britain puts it, "In western Europe, we are hanging on by our fingernails." In truth, he says, "Europe is no longer Christian." When the French political theorist Marcel Gauchet writes of recent European history as "characterized by the collapse of what remained of the religious pillars of heteronomy and the triumph of the metaphysical principle of human independence," he is not indulging in hyperbole.

Numbers drawn from the long-term European Values Study (EVS) and other research efforts underscore the degree to which Europe has abandoned its Christian heritage. For one thing, the pews of Europe's churches are often empty. In France, only one in twenty people now attends a religious service every week, and those few who do go to church tend to be elderly. Only 15 percent of Italians attend religious services weekly, and just 30 percent of Germans still go to church at least once a month. Indifference is widespread. A mere 21 percent of Europeans believe religion to be "very important." In France, arguably the most secular of Europe's nations outside of the formerly Lutheran countries of northern Europe, the percentage who believe religion to be "very important" is lower still, at slightly over 10 percent. As Cardinal Dionigi Tettamanzi, archbishop of Milan, lamented in the *New York Times* in October 2003, "The parishes tell me that there are children who don't know how to make the sign of the cross." Only Europe's growing Muslim population seems to exhibit any religious fervor, as Mark Steyn and others have observed.

True, few Europeans proclaim outright atheism, and a majority still call themselves Christians. But how many are Christian in anything but a nominal sense? Not only do Europeans not go to church very often; only about 40 percent believe in heaven and only half that percentage in hell. The idea of sin is vanishing from the European mind. Just 57 percent of Spaniards, 55 percent of Germans, 40 percent of the French, and roughly 30 percent of Swedes now believe in the concept.

Post-Christian Europe has unsurprisingly sunken progressively deeper into moral relativism. Assessing the EVS's findings, Romir, a Russian public opinion and market research group, notes that in most European countries, "Many people believe that there are no absolutely unambiguous rules on what is good and evil that apply to everyone, irrespective of the circumstances." The EVS also shows that a more radical view—that good and evil depend entirely on cultural and historical circumstances—is gaining currency across the continent, with only Poland and Malta resisting the trend. "Moral relativism would therefore appear to be predominant in Europe," Romir notes. This is particularly true when it comes to sexual and bioethical concerns. Only when it comes to tax-evasion and bribery do Europeans retain a relatively straightforward, "old-fashioned" sense of right and wrong.

Empty pews, aging believers, indifference—almost everything about western Europe's religious life conveys the sense of exhaustion. Nearly every trend is moving in the direction identified by Gauchet, away from any strong sense of religious identification and toward greater individualism and secularism. The European Union's refusal to include any reference to Europe's Christian heritage in its proposed constitution, despite the protests of the Vatican and various European Christian groups, is historically absurd, given Christianity's significant contribution to the development of the idea of human rights. But it hardly came as a surprise.

Religious America

In the United States, of course, the facts are quite different. The religious scene here is not desiccated but characterized by the presence of robust faith communities and intense spiritual thirst. More than 60 percent of Americans (nearly thrice the European percentage) claim that "religion plays a very important role" in their lives. More than 80 percent of Americans (90 percent in some surveys) profess belief in God.

America boasts countless houses of worship. *U.S. News & World Report* points out that there are "more churches, synagogues, temples, and mosques per capita in the United States than in any other nation on earth: one for about every 865 people." And those houses overflow with worshipers. A full 22 percent of America's 159 million Christians (three-fourths of the adult population) say they attend religious services more than once a week, and almost three-quarters of Christians attend at least once or twice a month. More people in the United States attend religious services on any given weekend than watch football, believe it or not.

There are television and radio stations which offer religious programming around the clock. Most bookstores feature well-stocked religion sections, and many of the books shelved there sell briskly, some even becoming bestsellers. The number of explicitly antireligious books, like Sam Harris's *Letter to a Christian Nation*, hitting the shelves these days only underscores the pervasiveness of American religiosity. Public figures from presidents to basketball stars openly thank God for granting them spiritual strength or success.

America also appears in some ways to be getting more religious, not less. The Pew Research Center recently found that the number of Americans who "agree strongly" with three fundamental tenets of faith—the existence of God, the reality of Judgment Day, and the importance of prayer—has risen by as much as ten points over the last four decades. Fifteen years ago, the *Economist* points out, two-fifths of American Protestants described themselves as "born again"—signaling a strong embrace of Christ as personal savior. That percentage has now climbed to more than half. Born-again Christians now make up 39 percent of America's adult population. Furthermore, four out of five Americans say they have "experienced God's presence or a spiritual force," and 46 percent maintain that they have such experiences often. "People are reaching out in all directions in their attempt to escape from the seen world to the unseen world," pollster George Gallup Jr. tells *U.S. News*. "There is a deep desire for spiritual moorings—a hunger for God."

Of course, secularizing forces do exist in the United States. America's highly educated, often left-leaning elites are every bit as secular as the most disenchanted Europeans. As Peter Berger says of this elite, "Its members are relatively thin on the ground," but they control "the institutions that provide the 'official' definitions of reality, notably the education system, the media of mass communication, and the higher reaches of the legal system." These elites have wrought secularizing changes in law and culture over the last several decades—using the courts to ban creche displays from public property and to end prayer or religious instruction of any kind in public schools, for example. However, they have yet to persuade the majority of Americans to embrace a secular worldview themselves.

Europe's Point of Departure

How are we to explain this divergence in religiosity within the liberal democratic universe? One thing that cannot help us is the "secularization theory" once popular among sociologists. In Berger's words, that theory posits that "modernization necessarily leads to a decline of religion, both in society and in the minds of individuals." Secularization theory now seems implausible, as Berger, a former proponent, acknowledges. If modernity inevitably brings secularism, a "disenchantment of the world," then how is it that the United States—the modern nation par excellence—is so religious? Nor is secularization increasing in modernizing areas of the world, from Latin America to the Middle East, Berger explains. Europe today seems more the exception than the rule when it comes to religious belief.

A more plausible explanation points to the very dissimilar histories of how democracy arrived in America and in Europe. The European democratic tradition, the model for which originated in the French Revolution, has been hostile to religion from its inception, and religion, especially the Catholic Church, had until recently been hostile to it in return. In America, however, democracy and religion have, mostly, been allies. Alexis de Tocqueville understood clearly this divergence between Europe and America. "Among us," he wrote of the French in *Democracy in America*, "I had seen the spirit of religion and the spirit of freedom almost always move in contrary directions." In America, by contrast, Tocqueville found the spirits of religion and democracy "united intimately with one another: they reigned together on the same soil."

Tocqueville believed religion would necessarily lose any battle with democracy if it sought to oppose it outright. The "providential" advance of the "equality of conditions" in the modern world, he argued, made some form of democracy a fate, not a choice. Yet such an accommodation with democracy would have been hard to justify or even imagine for the Catholic Church and its supporters in the late eighteenth and nineteenth centuries.

Before the French Revolution, one could find within the ranks of the Catholic Church advocates of social and democratic reform as well as adherents of the old regime. The gathering of the three estates that began the revolutionary process in France could not have taken place without the support of many clergy. But the French revolutionaries, influenced in particular by Rousseau's notion of the "general will," conceived of democracy in a way that imposed no limits on its power—putting man in God's place as sovereign and master of reality. Throw off superstition and the old power structures, let Reason rule, and the perfectibility of man was possible—or so the revolutionaries believed. The idea of original sin was for them a myth invented by a benighted and prudish church to darken minds and maintain social control.

The revolutionaries' ambitions meant they had to eradicate the spiritual and institutional power of the church, since it made rival claims for human allegiance. "These priests . . . must die because they are out of place, interfere with the movement of things, and will stand in the way of the future," Georges Danton pronounced in a spirit typical of the revolutionaries.

In pursuing their radical ends, as scholars such as J. L. Talmon and Furet have shown, France's revolutionaries became proto-totalitarians. As early as November 1789, the first year of upheaval, they nationalized church property and soon boarded up convents and monasteries. They mandated that all clerics would henceforth be state officials, subject to election by the laity—including nonbelievers. The violence escalated as the revolution advanced: churches were torched, altars desecrated, religious libraries wrecked, and priests and nuns violated by being forced to marry and have sex. The Jacobin Reign of Terror of 1793 and 1794 saw even greater abuses. The revolutionaries sent scores of priests (and many others) to the guillotine. In a sacrilegious gesture, they moved the remains of Voltaire from his estate at Ferney to the Church of Sainte-Genevieve, which they renamed the Pantheon. Notre Dame Cathedral was transformed into the "Temple of Reason."

In response, the Catholic Church set itself resolutely against "progress, liberalism, and modern civilization," in the words of Pope Pius IX's infamous 1864 "Syllabus of Errors." The church became a symbol of resistance to democracy—a resistance that, as Tocqueville predicted, was doomed to fail against the "providential" movement of history toward democracy. It was not until Vatican II, in the mid-sixties, that the Catholic Church finally came to terms with democracy and began instead to claim historical responsibility for its emergence.

Meanwhile, the French Revolution, despite its enormous abuses of power and its failure to establish a viable political order, won an honored reputation not just among the French but among generations of Europeans. It became the symbol of light, the vanguard of political freedom against all the agents of the old order, including religion. The anticlerical spirit of the revolution, reinforced by school curricula and public traditions, has continued to typify European democracies, nowhere more so than in France itself—witness the bestselling books of the young radical philosopher Michel Onfray, such as *Traité d'athéologie*, which attack Christianity with blood-curdling rhetorical violence. These days, Onfray's success notwithstanding, Europe's secularism tends to be far less ferocious than in Robespierre's time. As Pierre Manent writes, European democracy no longer plans "to destroy the infamous thing"—that is, the church. It "consents to the presence in its bosom" of religious believers. But that is only because it was victorious in its struggle against Christianity. For many Europeans, to be a modern democrat means necessarily that one is also secular.

America's Point of Departure

In America, relations between religion and democracy developed very differently, indeed, in ways that have encouraged the flourishing of faith visible around the nation today. At first blush, this might appear surprising. The dominant view among scholars, at least until quite recently, has been that the American Revolution, like the French, was an expression of the secular Enlightenment—finding its inspiration in the commonsensical natural rights philosophy of John Locke. According to this view, the Constitution privatized religion, downgrading its public status permanently.

In Walter Berns's words, "The Constitution was ordained and established to secure liberty and its blessings, not to promote faith in God. Officially, religion was subordinate to liberty and it was to be fostered only with a view to securing liberty." This view obviously captures important truths about the American polity: The framers drew much insight from Locke and, more broadly, from the Anglo-Scottish Enlightenment, and they certainly wanted to avoid the religious strife that Europe had suffered. But it also neglects the degree to which a religious consciousness pervaded the founding era. Recent books and essays by Daniel Dreisbach, James Hutson, Philip Hamburger, Michael Novak, and others have helpfully redressed this imbalance. "The leaders of the American Revolution were not, like the leaders of the French Revolution, secularists," Novak writes in his book *On Two Wings.* "They did not set out to erase religion."

On the contrary: Novak reminds us that the very first act of the First Continental Congress in 1774 was an official prayer—a psalm read aloud to the congressmen by an Episcopal clergyman. The Declaration of Independence, he notes, takes the form of a traditional American prayer not all that different from the Mayflower Compact, speaking of God in four ways—Creator (the source of our "unalienable rights"), Judge, Lawgiver, and Providence—that are, with the exception of Lawgiver, unambiguously biblical. Early American political debates made frequent use of biblical references and language. One scholar, Donald Lutz, surveyed 3,154 citations made by the founders and discovered that more than one-third of them were to the Bible. Montesquieu and Blackstone followed with three hundred or so each, while Locke trailed far behind.

As Tocqueville emphasized, religion and democracy "reigned together" in America long before 1776. The colonies, populated by deeply devout religious dissenters, had nourished vibrant republican traditions. More to the point, unlike in Europe, where religion took the side of the established authorities in opposition to democracy, America's Puritan pulpits helped to ignite the American Revolution itself. John Adams extolled the Philadelphia ministers who "thunder and lighten every Sabbath" against George III's tyranny. "To the Pulpit, the Puritan Pulpit, we owe the moral force which won our independence," said John Wingate Thornton.

For the founders, religion did more than help the nation win independence. Successful self-government required moral virtues—self-control, self-reliance, and a disinterested concern for the commonweal—that only religion could provide, at least for the majority. (Some refined souls, with minds of "peculiar structure," George Washington conceded, could be moral without this aid.) Washington's Farewell Address praised religion as the "indispensable" support of the "dispositions and habits which lead to political prosperity." Benjamin Rush agreed, "The only foundation for a useful education in a republic is to be laid in religion. Without it there can be no virtue, and without virtue there can be no liberty, and liberty is the object and life of all republican governments."

Even Jefferson, the most secular of the founders, was no Danton. Whatever his private beliefs, the Virginian grasped the public importance of religion: "No nation has ever existed or been governed without religion. Nor can be." As president, he supported with public money the church services, including Christian communion, held in various public buildings in Washington, D.C., and he signed a treaty (ratified by the Senate) with the Kaskaskias Indians that mandated the provision of federal funds to maintain a Catholic church among them.

Inner Tensions

Some scholars have argued that the "natural rights" theory of the American founding is ultimately antagonistic toward

Jewish and Christian faith. By putting the individual and his free conscience at the heart of the social order, the argument runs, liberal society erodes the claims of duty made upon men and women by any transcendent order. Indifference toward religion, even a relativistic indifference to all human goods, say some, are the all but inevitable byproducts.

The founders would not have agreed. In speaking the Lockean language of the "natural rights of mankind" in the same breath as professing fealty to God, as they so often did, they clearly saw no contradiction. Indeed, they held that natural rights, including the right to religious liberty, found their ultimate source in God.

Whether there may be a serious tension where the founders mainly saw compatibility remains an open question, of course. Contemporary America may exhibit intense religious activity, but it also has its relativistic currents, its individualist tendencies, its prurient enthusiasms, its civility-eroding "rights talk." To blame these phenomena, which have grown powerful since the 1960s, solely on secular elites seems too easy, though those elites have surely played a major role in promoting them. It is far more likely that such phenomena represent permanent temptations for all modern democratic societies.

What can be said with more certainty is that the founders sought not to diminish and degrade religion but to help it flourish. And on that score, they succeeded. George Washington once said that a nation's "first transactions" form the "leading traits in its character." With regard to the relations between religion and democracy, at least, this dictum has held true both for America, a republic founded in deep religious convictions it still largely affirms, and for Europe, where democracy was forged against religion and citizens have become less and less pious.

A Free Market of Religions

America's lack of an established state church and its religious pluralism together may point to another, related reason why America has diverged from Europe in matters of faith. It was not Tocqueville but his Scottish predecessor Adam Smith who first described the process at work.

In his classic treatise of political economy, *The Wealth of Nations*, Smith argued for the creation of what one could call a religious market. Just as in the economic sphere monopoly breeds stagnation and decline while competition tends to encourage striving and generate wealth, Smith believed that established churches would lose their appeal over time since their clergymen, having no real incentive to make their message compelling to the population, would grow complacent. Religions facing competitive pressure, however, would work harder and thrive.

Several contemporary sociologists have developed a theory of "religious economy" that builds on Smith's original insight. "Monopolies damage religion," emphasizes Massimo Introvigne, director of the Center for Studies on New Religions in Turin, Italy, and a major proponent of the theory. "In a free market, people get more interested in the product. It is true for religion just as it is true for cars." If the "demand" for religion is assumed to be constant, Introvigne explains, the amount and intensity of religiosity a culture exhibits depend on "the quality and quantity of religion available."

On this view, the European tradition of established churches has contributed to the decrease in religiosity among Europeans. Religious pluralism, by contrast, has made America more religiously energetic. Contrast the shriveled spiritual life of Scandinavian countries that have established state churches (or of France, which has a culturally established church), with the thriving faith communities of the United States, where Christian denominations actively compete for believers. Sixteen percent of American adults say they have switched denominations, signaling an extraordinary religious striving not unlike the "creative destruction" that continuously roils the hypercompetitive American economy.

In fact, observes Rodney Stark, the leading "religious economy" theorist, America has provided ample confirming evidence for the theory. Not only has church attendance progressively risen over the course of American history; American religion, he explains, also has been more vibrant in America's pluralistic cities than in its smaller towns or the countryside. And it turns out that the "religious marketing" theory even holds for antiquity. State religions initially did well in the ancient world, but over time, protected from competition, they grew decadent and withered.

Religion and Conservatism

All this history and social theory can help us understand why America and Europe have taken such different paths concerning religion. But what are the political and cultural consequences of this divergence today?

The religious divide is unquestionably a major cause of the growing tension between Europe and the United States. "To Europeans, religion is the strangest and most disturbing feature of American exceptionalism," notes the *Economist* in a recent major survey of the United States. The article continues: "They worry that fundamentalists are hijacking the country. They find it extraordinary that three times as many Americans believe in the virgin birth as in evolution. They fear that America will go on a 'crusade' (a term briefly used by Mr. Bush himself) in the Muslim world or cut aid to poor countries lest it be used for birth control."

In December 2003, in New York, writer Ian Buruma moderated a public discussion between European and American intellectuals—including the British leftist Tariq Ali, French philosopher Bernard-Henri Levy, and American journalist Jane Kramer—on the growing "gap" between Europe and the United States. "All the commentators agreed on one thing: the role of religion in U.S. politics was an affront to European secularism," said Buruma.

What such European disquiet is really about is the sizable presence in America of religious conservatism—a presence that also troubles observers here, such as Andrew Sullivan, who warns against the power of "Christianists" who fuse politics and religion. Evangelical Protestants are the fastest growing religious demographic in America and now represent 30 percent of the adult population. The most religiously committed among them—those who attend church regularly and claim fidelity to biblical ideals—have tended to describe themselves as politically conservative (a higher percentage than among any other religious group), and they care deeply about social issues like abortion and homosexuality. Whether these conservative Christians derive their political and cultural views from their faith or embrace their religious orthodoxy because of their convictions is unclear. What is indisputable, though, is that their faith reinforces their cultural conservatism.

These religious conservatives profoundly shape American society. From views on family life to charitable work (including soup kitchens, prison and drug-rehabilitation programs, and welfare-to-work initiatives), homeschooling, the new media, and innumerable other activities, they are a transpolitical presence in almost every walk of American life. In this way, they continue indirectly to influence political society by helping to "regulate" national mores, even if not to the extent observed by Tocqueville 150 years ago.

But they are also politically active as Christians. First through Jerry Falwell's Moral Majority (founded in 1979) and then through the Christian Coalition (founded ten years later), conservative Christians have become a formidable political force, central to the Republican Party's national fortunes. Evangelicals gave George W. Bush roughly four out of every ten votes he received in the 2000 presidential election and 36 percent of his voters in 2004. White evangelicals today make up nearly a third of registered voters, up from just under 25 percent fifteen years ago.

Given their political heft, religious conservatives have unsurprisingly become a major—probably *the* major—influence on the Republican Party's approach to social policy. Mainstream media coverage both here and abroad of the "religious Right" tends to portray it as fanatical (Fox News is a major exception), but its primary mission has been defensive: "a reaction against the popular counterculture, against the doctrinaire secularism of the Supreme Court, and against a government that taxes them heavily while removing all traces of morality and religion from public education, for example, even as it subsidizes all sorts of activities and programs that are outrages against traditional morality," in Irving Kristol's summation. Opposition to abortion and stem-cell research, efforts to head off gay marriage, attempts to rein in the imperial judiciary—religious conservatives are major players in each of these causes. That the Republican Party is much more conservative than "conservative" parties in Europe, which tend to combine economic statism with liberal stances on moral controversies, is almost entirely attributable to the sizable number of Christian fundamentalists in America.

Religious conservatives have enjoyed a particularly receptive welcome at the Bush White House, and not just on domestic policy issues. Shortly after Bush took office, the *New York Times* reported, Christian leaders met with presidential advisor Karl Rove to press for American intervention in the interminable civil war in Sudan, a religious conflict between Muslims and Christians that has led to two million deaths over the last several decades and terrible repression of Christians. Previous administrations had largely ignored the conflict, but Rove promised action. As a result, the Bush administration not only mediated peace talks in Sudan, it also launched initiatives to combat AIDS and sex trafficking in the Third World, two other key human-rights concerns of conservative Christians. President Bush went so far as to include extensive comments on sex trafficking in his United Nations speech of September 2003.

George W. Bush himself is a faithful evangelical Christian. He refers to God often in his speeches and has acknowledged, "I'd still be drinking if it weren't for what Christ did in my life." Bush's morally charged post–September 11 talk of bringing terrorist "evildoers" to "justice" arguably finds its primary source in the currents of religious fundamentalism. Vigorous religious and moral assertions of this kind, while they resonate with many Americans, appall secular, relativistic Europeans—indeed, they are a chief reason Europeans find Bush, and America as a whole, so unsettling these days.

The Great Divide

What does the future hold for America and Europe regarding religion and its cultural and political effects? A few possibilities come to mind.

Religion has become a major fault line in American politics. Secularists are sufficiently influential to have all but captured the Democratic Party. If Americans never go to church, they pull the lever for Democrats by a two-to-one ratio; if they do attend regularly, they have tended to vote Republican by a two-to-one majority. Religion is now "the most powerful predictor of party [identification] and partisan voting intention," political scientist Thomas Mann has observed.

Yet if secularizing forces exist, they are not welcomed by most Americans. According to a recent poll, 58 percent of American adults think that if you do not believe in God you cannot be moral. In addition, the secular Left's near monopoly over the institutions of information and opinion has begun to crack over the last half-decade or so, thanks to new media outlets in talk radio, cable television, the Internet, and publishing that have allowed religious and right-of-center viewpoints to get a much wider hearing in public debate, a development that I chronicled in my 2005 book *South Park Conservatives.* This greater diversity of media opinion, I belive, will reinforce America's religiosity.

As for Europe, it is possible to imagine a religious resurgence there, perhaps radiating outward from still-faithful and soon-to-be-powerful Poland. Rocco Buttiglione argues, to my mind persuasively, that European modernity, in its secular humanism, leaves men and women cut off from "an essential dimension of their being—the Absolute—and thus confronted with the worst diminution of their being." Such diminution is, over the long haul, existentially unbearable for "theotropic" beings (to use Irving Kristol's description of our human nature).

Yet a revival does not seem imminent. The rift between a religious America and a secular Europe is thus likely to widen in the years ahead, with unpredictable consequences for the democratic world as a whole.

5

A Brief History of Judicial Activism

Nothing rattles the American Left so completely as the specter of a conservative Supreme Court, and no wonder. Over the last half-century, sympathetic judges have handed the Left "progressive" policy victories that the voting booth wouldn't deliver. It is this liberal judicial legacy—on everything from affirmative action to abortion—that the Left fears a conservative bench will sweep away. Haunted by the doomsday scenario of a Supreme Court dominated by legal minds like Samuel Alito, Antonin Scalia, and Clarence Thomas, the Democrats and their allies will continue to fight with every means they can muster to block the appointment of conservative justices.

What liberals fear is a conservative judicial philosophy called "originalism," which holds that judges must base their rulings on the Constitution's text and structure, as the framers understood it, and they must interpret statutes to mean what they say. Very different from the activist and creative jurisprudence that has prevailed for the last half-century, this approach, which was the framers' accepted view of judging, would never have permitted the kind of expansive policy-making through which the Court has produced some of the Left's most cherished victories. An originalist Court could even overturn some of those victories, since they are so clearly unanchored in the Constitution.

Regardless of your view of the specific policies at issue, it is vital to America's democratic capitalist future that the originalists win this battle for the courts: the Supreme Court's politicized role in recent decades is corroding the self-government at the heart of American constitutionalism. In a democracy, voters, not unelected judges, decide the momentous questions. When the Supreme Court forces its policy preferences on the American people without the clear warrant of a constitutional text, as has happened often in the last fifty years, it is acting more as an "anti-democratic Caesar" than as the impartial referee it is supposed to be, in Justice Scalia's view. Moreover, by politicizing constitutional law, the Court has weakened the rule of law that is the bedrock of our constitutional form of government. As Justice Thomas notes, if law is just politics, "then there are no courts at all, only legislatures, and no Constitution or law at all, only opinion polls." And shouldn't our legislatures be elected?

The Original Originalists

It's worth understanding how our courts got into this mess, so we can see how imperative it is to get them out. The government by judiciary we now have is not what our founding fathers had in mind. The original originalists, they imagined that a life-tenured, independent judiciary would merely interpret the law as the people's elected representatives made it—including the supreme law embodied in the Constitution. But they would have no right to create law. As Alexander Hamilton explained in *The Federalist*: "The courts must declare the sense of the law, and if they should be disposed to exercise WILL instead of JUDGMENT, the consequence would equally be the substitution of their pleasure to that of the legislative body." For the framers, in other words, judicial lawmaking was akin to tyranny, and the proper solution was impeachment.

The Supreme Court took on the awesome powers it wields today with three big cases that occurred at intervals of half a century. Very briefly, the first was the 1857 *Dred Scott* decision, which concerned a Missouri slave, Scott, whose owner had taken him into parts of the Louisiana Territory where the federal government had banned slavery. Back home, Scott sued, saying that his stay in a free territory made him a free man, on the "once free, always free" principle that most Southern courts acknowledged. The Supreme Court, headed by Roger Taney and dominated by Southerners, ruled seven to two that Scott couldn't be free, in part because the Constitution did not give Congress the right to bar slavery in the federal territories (or anywhere else). In other words, the painstakingly negotiated Missouri Compromise of 1820, in which Congress had admitted Missouri as a slave state but made slavery illegal in other parts of the Louisiana Territory—a political deal that preserved the Union for nearly four decades—was unconstitutional. The ruling helped ignite the Civil War.

What makes *Dred Scott* the prototype of today's judicial activism is its radical rewriting of the Fifth Amendment's due process clause, which states that no person shall be "deprived of life, liberty, or property, without due process of law"— meaning, according to ancient legal tradition, simply that the authorities had to follow legally proper procedures in applying the law. In *Dred Scott*, the Court declared that any federal law that deprived a citizen of his slaves would *in itself* violate due process. This notion of "substantive" due process—that government can't deprive citizens of certain property or certain liberties without violating due process by the very act of doing so—"has enabled judges to do more freewheeling lawmaking than any other," says Scalia.

Lochnerizing the Constitution

You would think that after its war-fomenting foray into politics, the Court would have left legislating to legislators. But no: from the late 1890s until the mid-1930s, it again marshaled the substantive due process concept to make, rather than interpret, law. This time, the Court injected into the due process clause (not just of the Fifth Amendment but also of the post–Civil War Fourteenth Amendment, which applied it to the states) a natural right to the "freedom of contract" claimed by the nation's rising business class. This "substance"—this liberty that could be taken away by *no* legitimate due process—was more morally defensible than slaveholding, but the interpretive sleight of hand used to "discover" a protection that wasn't in the Constitution was the same as that used in *Dred Scott.* The 1905 *Lochner* case symbolizes this period in constitutional history: it struck down, on the substantive due process grounds that it violated freedom of contract, a New York law that limited bakers' workweeks to sixty hours for health reasons—only one of hundreds of federal and state social welfare laws, including early New Deal initiatives, that couldn't get past the courts during these decades. "Like its even more unseemly ancestor *Dred Scott,*" observe legal thinkers Eugene Hickok and Gary McDowell, "*Lochner* helped set in motion the mechanics of government by judiciary."

Just as *Dred Scott* helped precipitate a war, "*Lochner*izing" the Constitution provoked a constitutional crisis. Frustrated by the Supreme Court's thwarting of New Deal legislation, President Franklin D. Roosevelt threatened in 1937 to "pack" the Court with six additional judges who shared his politics. The justices averted the threat by mending their high-handed ways.

The *Brown* Watershed

The modern era of judicial activism opened in 1954 with one of the most celebrated Supreme Court decisions ever: *Brown v. Board of Education*. In *Brown*, a unanimous Court, led by new chief justice Earl Warren, ruled that state-mandated school segregation violated the Fourteenth Amendment's injunction that no state may "deny to any person within its jurisdiction the equal protection of the laws." *Brown* struck down a shameful injustice; but *how* the Court erased the color line had deeply troubling implications.

The Court faced two big constitutional obstacles to ending school segregation. First: precedent. The infamous 1896 *Plessy v. Ferguson* decision had held that segregation in the provision of government services didn't violate equal protection, as long as the separate facilities were equivalent. This "separate but equal" precedent wasn't insurmountable, but the Court, following the legal tenet of *stare decisis*–that a decision in one case should apply in subsequent cases–doesn't reverse itself lightly. Still, even seventy years of settled law could be thrown out the window if the Court could show that the original purpose of the equal protection clause barred school segregation.

Sadly, this approach also seemed to meet a brick wall. The aim of the Reconstruction Congress that had adopted the Fourteenth Amendment in 1868, most legal scholars agreed, had been to protect newly emancipated blacks from violations of their basic civil rights–such as access to courts or the ability to buy and sell property–not to grant them political rights (the vote) or social rights (such as desegregated education). After all, the same legislators who devised the equal protection clause funded Washington's segregated schools without qualms. Precedent and history—key pillars of jurisprudence—thus did not support the view that the Constitution demanded desegregation. Legal historian Alfred Kelly, who helped the NAACP lawyers prepare the *Brown* brief, later admitted, "I didn't see a good argument that might be available to us."

But the Warren Court wasn't going to let these difficulties impede it from doing justice. "We cannot turn the clock back to 1868, when the [Fourteenth] amendment was adopted, or even to 1896 when . . . *Plessy* was written," Warren's opinion for the Court asserted. Instead, the Court relied on social psychology research, which purported to show that segregation harmed the self-esteem of black schoolchildren and made it tougher for them to learn. Therefore, the Court said, "separate" wasn't "equal" in education, regardless of what the Fourteenth Amendment's framers intended or the *Plessy* Court believed.

However well-intentioned, this argument advanced no legal reason to reach its holding. "As a matter of principled constitutional law," says Northwestern legal scholar Stephen Presser, "the *Brown* opinion is almost certainly indefensible."

Nevertheless, *Brown*, acclaimed by the nation's opinion-leaders, became a powerful spur to future judicial lawmakers, who now would seek to advance the values of liberal rather than business elites (as had been the case in *Lochner*) in order to bring about social change. From *Brown* onward, the equal protection clause of the Fourteenth Amendment became a powerful engine of judicial power. In later decisions, the Court would take equal protection even further beyond the intention of its framers to encompass new legal guarantees not just for blacks but also for women, homosexuals, and other disfavored groups.

The Judge as Civil Rights Hero

In addition, *Brown* led to a shift in elites' perception of what made for a good judge and a good judgment. By the time the sixties cultural revolution was in full swing, writes Harvard law professor Mary Ann Glendon, "judges began to be praised for qualities that once would have been considered problematic: compassion rather than impartiality, boldness rather than restraint, creativity rather than craftsmanship, and specific results regardless of the effect on the legal order as a whole."

The heroic new judge drew inspiration from a doctrine called "the Living Constitution," which held, as Justice William Brennan put it, that "[t]he genius of the Constitution rests not in any static meaning it might have had in a world that is dead and gone, but in the adaptability of its great principles to cope with current problems and current needs." In practice, the concept of the Living Constitution could be employed to bring about epochal social changes whenever judges like Brennan believed that justice demanded them. Legislators, for their part, began to refuse to deal with contentious issues; the Supremes would be sure to take them off their hands.

Amazingly, the Court was even able to use *Brown*—an antidiscrimination decision—as the basis of a new rationale for government to discriminate by race. After all, *Brown* hadn't overturned *Plessy* or endorsed Justice John Harlan's famous dissent in *Plessy* that "[o]ur Constitution is color blind, and neither knows nor tolerates classes among citizens." So even though the Warren Court, citing *Brown*, desegregated everything from city golf courses to public swimming pools, the decision had never ruled that equal protection forbade racial discrimination by government.

In the last of its desegregation decisions, *Loving v. Virginia*, the Warren Court established the legal test currently used to identify lawful racial discrimination. Under the Living Constitution, race is a "suspect classification"; courts must give any laws or government actions that use race as a criterion "strict scrutiny," which means that they must determine first that such laws are narrowly focused to serve only a compelling state interest and none other, and second that there are no colorblind alternatives available. This test, observes political scientist Richard Morgan, is an "intellectual disaster"—a permanent invitation for judges to legislate from the bench, since its criteria are "essentially political judgments about wise public policy."

These highly subjective criteria are objectionable enough, but—worse still—the Court has used them to ride roughshod over Congress's explicit intentions, as expressed in the landmark 1964 Civil Rights Act. This exemplary legislation not only forbade segregated public schools but also made it illegal for government, or any employer engaged in interstate commerce or receiving government contracts, "to discriminate against any individual . . . because of such individual's race, color, religion, sex, or national origin." The act also required government and private employers to make a special effort to hire qualified minorities and to give them training if necessary to get them up to speed—"affirmative action," as it later came to be called. Such special efforts, the law clearly stated, did not mean that there was to be preferential treatment, quotas, or reverse discrimination. Period.

But quotas and reverse discrimination are exactly what the Supreme Court brought about. In decisions from *Griggs* in 1971 to *Bakke* and *Weber* in the late seventies to *Metro Broadcasting* in 1990, the Court turned inside out the meaning and intent of the Civil Rights Act. The Court, rejecting a "literal interpretation" of the act's words, ruled that the law actually didn't prevent racial preferences in the hiring and promoting of blacks, that universities could use race as a factor in admissions decisions, and that judges could even impose strict racial hiring and promotion quotas on employers who had discriminated against blacks in the past. (Over time, an estimated 70 percent of the U.S. population, including women, the elderly, and various racial and ethnic groups, became eligible for court-approved preferential treatment.) Though in more recent decisions the Supreme Court has narrowed the scope of its affirmative action policy, it still rules unpredictably on the question—in the 2003 *Grutter* decision making the idea of "diversity" a possible justification for preferences.

The Court tortured the Civil Rights Act with equal disregard for congressional intent in trying to speed up school desegregation. The act plainly stated that desegregation didn't mean assigning students to schools by race, and busing them there, to promote integration. But in *Green* (1968) and *Swann* (1971), the high court, now under Chief Justice Warren Burger, allowed district courts to mandate the busing of students to achieve racial balance. Whatever the worth of policies like busing and affirmative action, the post-*Brown* Court, in imposing them on a citizenry that largely views them as unjust, was doing exactly what Hamilton said it could not lawfully do under our Constitution: exercising will, not judgment.

The moral rightness of *Brown*'s result, however, has meant that critics of the Living Constitution doctrine constantly must deal with the charge that, if they object to *Brown*'s jurisprudence—its means rather than its end—they must be racists. What makes this charge doubly absurd is that the American people, not the judges, finally sent Jim Crow packing. As Wallace Mendelson and other historians point out, widespread segregation in the South continued after *Brown* until Congress passed the 1964 Civil Rights Act and the 1965 Voting Rights Act and Elementary and Secondary Education Act. Thereafter, says Mendelson, "revolutionary changes followed"–sparked, as is appropriate, by the legislation of the people's elected representatives, not the dictates of unelected judges.

Judicial originalists have no trouble supporting *Brown*'s outcome without embracing the Living Constitution dogma. In Judge Robert Bork's view, whatever the Fourteenth Amendment's framers might have thought about the compatibility of segregation with the explicit ideal of equality animating the amendment, it was painfully obvious by the 1950s that "separate" facilities for blacks always were inferior. Recent research by Michael W. McConnell, another leading originalist and a Bush appeals-court appointee, shows that, shortly after the Fourteenth Amendment's ratification, a majority of those who voted for the measure in Congress believed that it was incompatible with state-sponsored segregation. Originalist Clarence Thomas, going further, maintains that each of the post–Civil War amendments–the Thirteenth (banning slavery), the Fourteenth, and the Fifteenth (extending the vote to blacks)–embodies the magnificent vision of the Declaration of Independence that "all men are created equal": equal protection, interpreted against this backdrop, renders unconstitutional not only segregation but any laws that take race into account. Harlan was right, says Thomas: the Constitution is colorblind.

Other originalists disagree. Legal scholar Terry Eastland objects: "No majority of the Supreme Court has ever said, either explicitly or by implication, that the Constitution is colorblind." And because *Brown* didn't overrule *Plessy*, and the Court went on to use that decision to turn the antidiscrimination 1964 Civil Rights Act into a warrant for government racial preferences, other originalists of Eastland's stamp believe that those who seek a colorblind Constitution should work to pass a constitutional amendment blocking government from distinguishing by race. Argues Richard Morgan: "This would finally complete the work of Reconstruction, align the text of the Constitution with our national ideals, and bury Jim Crow the way he should have been buried in the first place—by votes in legislative assemblies."

New Rights for Criminals

If no one disagrees with the antisegregation result of *Brown*, many disagree strongly with the anti-law-enforcement result of another of the Warren Court's forays into legislating from the bench. Driven by the 1960s elite's suspicion of police authority, the Court conjured out of the Living Constitution completely new procedural rights for the criminally accused. These novel rights revolutionized the way the nation dealt with crime and helped fuel the crime explosion that began in the mid-1960s.

In *Mapp v. Ohio* (1961), the Warren Court rewrote the Constitution to force state courts to exclude from criminal cases any evidence that police obtained in an improper search, even if the cops' error was inadvertent and tiny. This "exclusionary rule," derived from the Fourth Amendment's protection against unreasonable search and seizure, had never applied to states before 1961. The majority in *Mapp* pulled off this remarkable extension of the exclusionary rule's scope by "incorporating" the Fourth Amendment guarantees, which apply to the federal government, into the rights protected by the due process clause of the Fourteenth Amendment, which applies to the states. This "nationalization" of the Bill of Rights, which began in the 1920s but principally occurred in the 1960s, "did more than anything else to make the Supreme Court the most powerful voice in the land in defining the rights of the American people," opines law scholar Scott Douglas Gerber.

Mapp wasn't the only new impediment the Court put in law enforcement's way. In 1966, it handed down in a five-to-four ruling the famous *Miranda* decision. "You have the right to remain silent; anything you say can and will be held against you in a court of law; you have the right to an attorney, and if you cannot afford one, one will be appointed for you"—anybody who's ever watched a cop show knows the warnings. Here the Court took the Fifth Amendment's rule against self-incrimination, which previously had applied only to courtroom testimony, and—with breathtaking interpretive license—extended it to cover statements and confessions made during police interrogations.

Miranda brusquely threw out the centuries-old "voluntariness" test for confessions. Was a confession the result of an unconstrained choice? If yes, the test held, prosecutors could use it against the confessor; if not—if interrogators had coerced the confession—prosecutors couldn't use it. Justice John Marshall Harlan (grandson of the *Plessy* dissenter) excoriated the Court for replacing this test, "an elaborate, sophisticated, and sensitive approach to admissibility of confessions," with an inflexible, heavy-handed approach that, like *Mapp*, made it impossible to balance the rights of the accused against the competing values of finding the truth and protecting society.

Stung by two decades of public backlash for being more solicitous of criminals' rights than of public safety—and by research showing that these decisions had reduced the conviction rate among criminal suspects—the Supreme Court retreated slightly from its unwavering suspicion of law enforcement in the 1984 *Nix v. Williams* decision. There the Court said that prosecutors could legally introduce evidence that police had seized based on a bad warrant if the cops had, in good fath, thought it valid. Even so, in *Dickerson v. United States* (2000), the Rehnquist Court upheld *Miranda* by a seven-to-two majority. The Court rested its case not on the Constitution's text—how could it?—but on its own precedent and on the fact that *Miranda* "has become embedded in routine police practice to the point where the warnings have become part of our national culture," as Rehnquist's opinion for the Court explained. A dissenting Scalia, joined by Clarence Thomas, blasted the majority for maintaining the "power judging" that had foisted *Miranda* on police in the first place, in contravention of the Constitution's plain meaning.

Inverting the First Amendment

The Court has subjected the First Amendment to a stiff dose of "power judging" as well. It has used the amendment's religion clause—"Congress shall make no law respecting an establishment of religion, or prohibiting the free exercise thereof"—to erect a nearly impassable "wall of separation" between church and state, a wall that the framers never envisioned. Washington, as we have seen, thought religion "indispensable" to the "dispositions and habits which lead to political prosperity"—a view that seems to belong to a different universe from a 2000 Supreme Court ruling that a short, freely chosen, nonsectarian, and non-proselytizing prayer delivered by a student before a high school football game represented an unconstitutional establishment of religion.

The Court has also inverted the original meaning of the First Amendment's free speech clause, which the framers intended as a protection of political speech, not as a license for indecency and obscenity. As Supreme Court Justice Joseph Story, the early-nineteenth-century's leading constitutional authority, put it: "That this amendment was intended to secure to every citizen an absolute right to speak, or write, or print whatever he may please, without any responsibility, public or private, therefore, is a supposition too wild to be indulged in by any rational man." As late as 1942, a unanimous Court ruled that the First Amendment didn't protect obscene or lewd words because "such utterances are no essential part of any exposition of ideas, and are of such slight social value as a step to truth that any benefit that may be derived from them is clearly outweighed by the social interest in order and morality."

But all that began to change with the Court's 1971 *Cohen v. California* ruling, which threw out the disorderly conduct conviction of a man who had refused to take off a jacket emblazoned: FUCK THE DRAFT. Opined Justice Harlan, writing for the Court: "[O]ne man's vulgarity is another's lyric." *Cohen* and myriad decisions since have made it nearly impossible for communities to regulate any speech or image. In 2002, the Court struck down a law criminalizing "virtual" kiddie porn, including computer-created images of kids having sex.

The high court protects pornography, but it has curtailed the political speech essential to democratic debate which it was the original purpose of the First Amendment to protect. In *Buckley v. Valeo* (1976) and *Nixon v. Shrink Missouri Government PAC* (2000), the Court upheld legislation that, seeking to stamp out corruption or even the appearance of corruption, strictly limited political contributions. Now, telling someone he can't spend his money promoting his political views is a pretty clear-cut infringement of his political speech, exactly what the First Amendment is supposed to protect. Fortunately, there are some signs that the Roberts Court may be backing away from this line of decisions.

Penumbras and Emanations

Questions of sex have tempted the Court to bend and twist the Constitution almost as energetically as questions of race. *Roe v. Wade* (1973) is the most famous case in point. Whatever one's views about abortion, as jurisprudence *Roe* is undeniably—and embarrassingly—shoddy. In a fifty-one-page majority opinion by Justice Harry Blackmun that lacked any discernible legal reasoning, the Court based its ruling on the "privacy" right of married couples to use contraceptives. (It was in the 1965 *Griswold v. Connecticut* case that the Court had discovered this right in the "penumbras, formed by emanations," of the Bill of Rights.) This new guarantee of privacy, conjured up like a will-o'-the-wisp rising out of swamp gas, included an absolute right, protected by the due process clause of the Fourteenth Amendment, for all women to terminate pregnancy up until the third trimester—a penumbra formed by emanations indeed.

The dissent of Associate Justice William Rehnquist exposed *Roe*'s constitutional illegitimacy. When Congress adopted the Fourteenth Amendment, he noted, at least thirty-six state or territorial laws curbed abortion, and no one questioned their constitutional validity at the time. Many of those laws were still on the books in 1973. "The only conclusion possible from this history is that the drafters did not intend to have the Fourteenth Amendment withdraw from the States the power to legislate with respect to this matter," said Rehnquist. Given that history, as well as the Court majority's comical arguments, *Roe* was, as Justice Byron White's dissent put it, nothing more than "an exercise of raw judicial power."

In the 1992 *Casey* decision, the Court reached the furthest limit of judicial invention. In *Casey*, Justices Anthony Kennedy, Sandra Day O'Connor, and David Souter authored an opinion that defended a woman's right to end her pregnancy by rooting that right in a new concept of liberty. "At the heart of liberty [as protected by the due process clause]," the justices wrote, "is the right to define one's own concept of existence, of meaning, and of the mystery of human life." Not a word in the Constitution acknowledges such a right, of course. What could it possibly mean? If I am a Muslim, and my "concept of meaning" allows me multiple wives, do I have a constitutional right to have the state recognize my marriages as legal? If so, there go laws against polygamy. In a nation that values individualism and the pursuit of happiness, it is hard to imagine any law that wouldn't stand in the way of somebody's "concept of meaning."

Casey, legal scholars think, led to the 1996 *Romer* v. *Evans* decision, in which the Court struck down Colorado's democratically crafted constitutional provision that homosexuals and bisexuals should not get special rights beyond those granted to the rest of the citizenry. Such a provision, the Court argued, could only be based on irrational "animus" against homosexuals. Scalia's withering dissent spells out just how arrogantly antidemocratic the Court's reasoning was. "Since the Constitution of the United States says nothing about this subject [homosexual rights]," he argued, "it is left to be resolved by normal democratic means, including the democratic adoption of provisions in state constitutions. This Court has no business imposing upon all Americans the resolution favored by the elite class from which the Members of this institution are selected, pronouncing that 'animosity' toward homosexuality is evil." *Romer* also sparked a heated symposium in the respected, highbrow religious magazine *First Things*, in which several constitutional scholars, including Bork and Princeton legal philosopher Robert George, argued that the imperial judiciary that had delivered *Casey* and *Romer* had left religiously orthodox Americans and moral conservatives little recourse but civil disobedience to protect their values.

Afffirmative action and busing, new rights for the criminally accused, a First Amendment that protects virtual kiddie porn but not a nondenominational prayer before a school football game—these are just some of the major ways the federal judiciary has helped remake America since *Brown*. The Supreme Court has created due process rights for public school pupils facing disciplinary proceedings and for youths in the juvenile justice system; it has struck down as violations of equal protection state legislatures designed—like the Congress—with one population-based legislative chamber and another based on geographic boundaries; it has churned out a torrent of employment regulations—everything from rendering aptitude tests unconstitutional if they have a "disparate impact" on minorities to making it harder to fire people; it has overturned a state law banning partial-birth abortions, which even many abortion supporters consider infanticide; it has, most recently, banned the death penalty (which the Bill of Rights explicitly allows) for the mentally retarded. Cumulatively, these decisions have removed many of the most important moral and social issues from the political arena, shrinking the realm of self-government that America was founded to guarantee. "Day by day, case by case," laments Scalia, the judges are "busy designing a Constitution for a country I don't recognize."

Why the Originalists Are Right

Since these decisions have almost invariably pushed forward the Left's political agenda, it is no surprise that an entire industry has sprung up in the left-leaning academy to justify and advance the Living Constitution idea. The University of Chicago's Cass Sunstein, for instance, argues that the Constitution directs the judiciary to function as democracy's referee, deciding which choices of the people are what they *really* intend, and which are in some sense accidental and therefore nonbinding. Harvard's Laurence Tribe, author of a popular constitutional-law textbook, argues, like Justice Brennan, that the Constitution's grand principles must evolve with time to meet the changing needs of society. Judges supply the correct interpretation of those principles, not based on what the framers had in mind, but in accordance with the views of enlightened Americans—which today means the left wing of the Democratic party. Adherents of the Critical Legal Studies movement and its offshoots believe that jurisprudence merely expresses race or gender or economic power relations, rather than an effort to do objective, disinterested justice. Thus, creative interpretations of the Constitution that help improve the lot of the disenfranchised are the turnabout that is fair play.

Against such thinkers stands a much smaller band of originalists defending what Scalia has memorably called the "Enduring Constitution." Originalists argue that America adopted a *written* Constitution precisely because it was *not* intended to change over time. "Otherwise," Thomas points out, "we would have adopted the British approach of an unwritten, evolving constitution." Second, originalists believe that high-court judges must base their decisions on the Constitution's text and structure as originally understood. They also maintain that legal and constitutional texts have a limited range of meaning that judges can gloss rightly or wrongly; truth is not an obsolete concept in law. Finally, originalists think that judges can be impartial interpreters of the law. "In order to be a judge," Justice Thomas has written, "a person must attempt to exorcise himself or herself of the passions, thought, and emotions that fill any frail human being. He must become almost pure, in the way that fire purifies metal, before he can decide a case." Otherwise, the judge is but a politician. Though a minority view on campus, originalism has made some inroads even there, as is partly evidenced by the critical success of Princeton political scientist Keith Whittington's 2001 book, *Constitutional Interpretation*.

Originalism is the only jurisprudence fully compatible with our form of government. Even if one did subscribe to the odd, recent idea that jurists should be able to ignore or deconstruct the text and original meaning of the Constitution, Scalia asks, why, in our democracy, should judges be the people uniquely entitled to determine society's needs? "It is simply not compatible with democratic theory that laws mean whatever they ought to mean, and that unelected judges decide what that is," he declares.

Cass Sunstein has come up with a theory that advocates institutionalizing these differences of opinion on the Supreme Court itself. In naming and confirming justices, argues Sunstein, who had advised the Democrats on these matters, the president and the Senate should ensure judicial pluralism, with appropriate representation of both approaches to jurisprudence. New York Democratic senator Chuck Schumer has taken Sunstein's argument a step further, now that a conservative president, who looks to Scalia and Thomas as his model judges, has been able to appoint two Supreme Court justices, thus changing the tenor of the Court and threatening, perhaps, ultimately to undo some of the Left's most cherished social gains. Let's just make the confirmation of judges a raw political fight, says Schumer, since the two parties have distinct and incompatible jurisprudential ideologies. Judging equals politics, plain and simple, on this view. With gladiatorial Schumerism on the scene, worries Stephen Presser, the threat to an independent judiciary "is probably more real now than it has been for three-quarters of a century"—since, that is, FDR's court-packing scheme.

Even from a narrowly partisan standpoint, though, the Left would be wise to think hard about whether it makes sense to reject originalism and treat the judiciary as a political war machine. After all, one can imagine a Court made up of real conservative activists who'd go beyond the Constitution to dismantle the welfare state completely, say, or to ban abortion (as opposed to letting states decide if they want to make it legal or to regulate it, as would happen if the Court simply overturned *Roe*). True, such an outcome is unlikely, since most conservative jurists are reflexively originalist in their jurisprudence. But the fact that it could happen should make liberals consider whether they might not be better off living under the Constitution our framers gave us, instead of one subject to constant political alteration. Originalism ultimately favors neither Left nor Right, but self-government.

President Ronald Reagan, swearing in Scalia in 1986, put it beautifully: the founding fathers, he said, "knew that the courts, like the Constitution itself, must not be liberal or conservative. The question was and is, will we have government by the people?" That is still the question.

III. Recto/Verso

6

The Antipolitical Philosophy of John Rawls

After the liberal philosopher John Rawls died of heart failure at the age of eighty-one in November 2002, obituaries and remembrances in prominent places testified to the man's greatness as a thinker. The *New York Times* led the way, publishing three notices of Rawls's passing: an obituary declaring that he "gave new meaning and resonance to the concepts of justice and liberalism"; a "Week in Review" piece arguing that he provided "intellectual spine to liberals seeking tough-minded defense of their instinct to take from the rich and give to the poor"; and a lengthy op-ed by Martha Nussbaum, who called him "the most distinguished philosopher of the twentieth century." The *Times*'s counterpart in England, the *Guardian*, asserted that Rawls had "rejuvenated and transformed the study of political philosophy." Rawls's Harvard colleague (and critic) Michael Sandel, writing for the *New Republic*, was almost reverential. Sandel recalled the phone call he received from Rawls upon first arriving at Harvard as a young professor: "This is John Rawls, R-A-W-L-S." For Sandel, "It was as if God himself had called to invite me to lunch and spelled his name just in case I didn't know who he was."

Nor was it just the Left that celebrated Rawls's achievements. The *Economist* obituary described his massive 1971 book *A Theory of Justice* as a "philosophical classic," though how that work's radical egalitarianism squares with the magazine's free-market ideals is hard to see. Even the unabashedly conservative *National Review Online* had good things to say, running a tribute by legal theorist Richard Epstein praising Rawls as "a genuine leader in philosophical and political thought."

The outpouring of acclaim confirmed Rawls's prestige and influence, both in the academy and beyond. *A Theory of Justice*, translated into roughly two dozen languages, has reportedly sold upward of 400,000 copies worldwide—an amazing figure for any philosophical work, let alone one so dense and dryly expressed. It would be only a slight exaggeration to say that since the 1970s, universities in the English-speaking world (and increasingly elsewhere) have transformed the teaching of political philosophy into an extended commentary on Rawls's thought. Thousands of essays and scores of books have appeared defending Rawls, criticizing Rawls, seeking to go beyond Rawls. A bibliography of this commentary, French philosopher Luc Ferry notes, would run eight hundred pages in length. Law professors also use Rawls's work as a touchstone, and some scholars have noted increasing evidence of his influence on judicial decisions. In 1999, President Bill Clinton awarded Rawls the Medal of Freedom. "Almost single-handedly," Clinton gushed, "John Rawls revived the disciplines of political and ethical philosophy."

Yet the adulation Rawls's work has met with—the years scholars have dedicated to the study of *A Theory of Justice*, and the numerous honors he has received—is all a bit surprising. For Rawls's thought is a long lesson in how not to think about politics. The egalitarian liberalism Rawls called justice would be unworkable in practice, even if it were desirable. His works do not speak to any recognizable political world and ignore almost completely the real dilemmas and tragedies of our time.

Biography of an Idea

John Borden Rawls was a private man who avoided publicity and gave only a couple of interviews during the course of his career. But some significant, if sketchy, biographical details have come to light in profiles undertaken by the British broadcaster Ben Rogers and political theorist Thomas Pogge. Born and raised in Baltimore, Rawls was the second of Anna and William Rawls's five sons. The Rawlses were wealthy: William Rawls was a tax attorney and constitutional authority, and his mother was the daughter of a prominent German family and president of the local chapter of the League of Women Voters. But successful as they were, the Rawlses did not escape tragedy. Two of John's younger brothers died as children—from illnesses they contracted from him. Rawls believed that he developed his lifelong stutter as a result of the guilt he felt over his brothers' deaths. His former student Joshua Cohen suggests that these sad early experiences ultimately found expression in *A Theory of Justice*'s emphasis on the "unmerited contingencies" of life. Why did Rawls live while his brothers died?

After attending the Episcopalian Kent School in Connecticut, Rawls entered Princeton University in 1939, where, under the influence of Wittgenstein student Norman Malcolm, he first became interested in political philosophy. Upon graduating in 1943, Rawls went to war as a private in the army, seeing active duty in the Pacific. While he was stationed there, the United States dropped the atomic bomb on Hiroshima. Rawls would, much later, write an article for *Dissent* condemning the bombing, one of the few occasions on which he descended from the empyrean of theory to discuss real-world affairs. Once again, Cohen suggests, Rawls believed he had benefited from an unmerited contingency: Had the United States not destroyed Hiroshima, he might have fought in Japan and perhaps lost his life.

Rawls returned to Princeton in 1946 to pursue a Ph.D. in moral and political philosophy. By 1949, the year he married painter Margaret Fox and finished his dissertation (on character and moral knowledge), he had already conceived of writing a book on justice. After stints at Cornell University and the Massachusetts Institute of Technology, and the publication of his first important essay on the idea of justice in 1957, he joined the Harvard University philosophy faculty in the early 1960s and quickly became a respected teacher. His lectures on the history of moral philosophy from Hume to Hegel, edited for publication by Barbara Herman, were particularly popular with students. In 1979, he became a "University Professor" at Harvard, the school's highest teaching post. Rawls officially retired in 1991 but continued teaching until 1995, when ill health made it too burdensome.

Justice as Fairness

The widespread notion—Ben Rogers terms it an "academic legend"—that Rawls "rejuvenated political philosophy" with *A Theory of Justice* is something of a myth. After all, the two decades or so that preceded the book's appearance saw the publication of Hannah Arendt's *Origins of Totalitarianism*, Raymond Aron's *Peace and War*, Isaiah Berlin's essays on freedom, Friedrich Hayek's *Constitution of Liberty*, Bertrand de Jouvenel's *Sovereignty*, Michael Oakeshott's *Rationalism in Politics*, and Leo Strauss's *Natural Right and History*—hardly a fallow field of political thought.

It is true, though, that Rawls's six-hundred-page tome, twenty years in the making, broke with the then dominant tendency within analytic philosophy to dismiss ethical and political reflection as basically meaningless. People had their value preferences, analytic philosophers said, and that was that. All philosophy could sensibly do was to analyze the use of language and the meaning of terms. Rawls's far grander aim in *A Theory of Justice* was in line with the great tradition of political philosophy: to come up with normative principles for evaluating political institutions and for guiding public life. "Justice is the first virtue of social institutions, as truth is of systems of thought," proclaimed Rawls at the outset of the book. "A theory however elegant and economical must be rejected or revised if it is untrue; likewise laws and institutions no matter how efficient and well-arranged must be reformed or abolished if they are unjust."

Rawls labeled his imposing theory "justice as fairness." He began with the notion of a preexisting moral sense, an "intuitive conviction" about freedom and equality, that he assumed we all share: "Each person possesses an inviolability founded on justice that even the welfare of society as a whole cannot override." Thus, no utilitarian calculus that sacrifices the rights of some for the greater benefit of the majority can be morally legitimate. But Rawls also claimed that our intuitions about what it means to be free and equal go much further. Individuals' chances in life should not suffer because of things beyond their control—an abusive or impoverished family background, or a violent neighborhood, or their skin color, or sex, or even their lack of genetic gifts like good looks or talent. It is society's obligation to ensure that unmerited contingencies affect our opportunities as little as possible. As Allan Bloom once said of Rawls's philosophy, we have not only rights to "life, liberty, and the pursuit of happiness," but the right to *be* happy, too.

The Original Position

To model these intuitions, and to deepen them, Rawls turned to the venerable tradition of the social contract. Rawls's social contract, like those of Hobbes and Locke, is hypothetical: Determining whether an arrangement of institutions is just or unjust requires asking if that arrangement would result from a contract made under fair conditions. But Rawls's version of the state of nature—"the original position," as he called it—is quite different from the dangerous precivilized condition described by earlier social contract thinkers, where life is "nasty, brutish, and short," as Hobbes famously put it. For the original contractarians, the state of nature allowed us to see man's nature unvarnished—asocial, selfish, driven by fear of sudden death, wary of potentially deadly neighbors. The contractual government that the raw men of the state of nature invest with authority has as its sole purpose security and social peace.

Rawls's original position, by contrast, says little about human nature. It describes a perfectly benign place in which perfectly reasonable, self-interested people are able to choose the principles of justice that will organize society free of the fear of death that disturbs Hobbes's or Locke's state of nature. To make sure the social architects in the original position choose justly, Rawls places them behind a "veil of ignorance," which magically strips them of any advantage they might possess over others—even of everything that makes them different from one another.

Behind the moral veil, an individual does not know his talents, his skin color, his family background, his character, his religious or other beliefs, or much of anything else about himself. All he knows is that certain "primary goods"—money, opportunities, various freedoms—are necessary for a successful life, and that the cooperation of others will help him meet his needs. Since the veiled person realizes that he might not possess natural advantages but instead be talentless, ugly, stupid, and burdened with a lousy family, Rawls argues that he will rationally adopt a risk-minimizing strategy in choosing his principles of justice, so that even if he winds up losing in life's lottery, his position will be as good as it can be.

Those in the original position, Rawls explains, would embrace two principles for designing a just society. The first, "equal liberty," is based on John Stuart Mill's principle of liberty. Everyone must have an equal right to the most extensive basic liberties consistent with the guarantee of the same liberties for all—rights to vote, to free speech, to association, and other civil liberties. Government is to remain neutral about rival understandings of the good life, but it must guarantee that liberties are equally distributed. The second, "difference" principle stipulates that social and economic inequalities are permissible only if they are to the greatest benefit of the "least advantaged" or "worst off," and if they are "attached to positions and offices open to all." Strict egalitarianism is the default position. The two principles cannot be traded off: sacrificing equal liberties for an increase in material well-being is unacceptable.

Many observers have regarded the Rawlsian concept of "justice as fairness" merely as constituting a defense of the modern capitalist welfare state. In truth, Rawls came to believe that even an expansive welfare state permits too much inequality to deserve our full support. In the final summation of his theory, *Justice as Fairness*, Rawls maintained that only a "property-owning democracy or a 'liberal socialism' that used government or judicial power to prevent a small part of society from controlling the economy, and indirectly, political life as well" would meet the criteria for justice. Since people's natural differences and choices inexorably generate new inequalities, government would need to intervene constantly and extensively in economic life to make sure those inequalities directly benefited the worst off, and if they did not, to stamp them out. To equalize liberties, government would, for example, finance all elections, so that money would not be a factor in their outcomes. All must "have a fair opportunity to hold public office and to affect the outcome of elections," Rawls writes. Similarly, a just society would need to regulate freedom of speech and the press (though not the content of speech) in order to ensure fair access to the media. The state looms large in Rawls's scheme. It is the muscular arm that makes things right, which for Rawls meant assuring not equality of opportunity but equality of results.

Later Revisions

Rawls happily described himself as a monomaniac, and he returned to his two principles repeatedly in subsequent works, responding to critics, glossing arguments, tinkering and amending. Rawls's biggest shift came in response to the charge, made by "communitarian" theorists like Michael Walzer and Michael Sandel, that his theory rested on a controversial, neo-Kantian view of the good—a secular vision of man as an autonomous chooser of moral alternatives, free from all preexisting moral ties and duties. Most of what we value, the communitarians maintained, is not chosen but given to us by our communities, which constantly need strengthening. Rawls's individualism, it was argued, reinforced all those relativizing tendencies in modern culture that undermined the sense of community.

In a series of essays, revised and published in book form as *Political Liberalism* (1993), Rawls recast his theory, saying that justice as fairness, *pace* the critics, was not an attempt to articulate an enduring truth about man but instead a reflection on the "traditions of a modern democratic state." Rawls's two principles of justice offered the political basis for an "overlapping consensus" among the myriad visions of the good life at work in a pluralistic society. Justice as fairness was not a blow against community, then, but rather the highest moral expression of the liberal ideal of community.

Rawls also sought to extend his theory to international society. In his 1999 book *The Law of Peoples*, Rawls posited a modified original position for international justice: Its choosers would be representatives of "peoples," not individuals. The agreement these representatives reach behind the veil of ignorance approves of liberal constitutional regimes as well as "decent" nonliberal regimes. The North Koreas of the world would receive no admission to the community of nations. (The unpleasant regimes owe their unpleasantness to accidental factors such as poverty or corrupt leadership; in the Rawlsian view, peoples never act badly of their own will.)

The decent peoples, Rawls argued, should act as if a worldwide "Society of Peoples" already existed and set an example for those who might join it in the future. This means that for liberal and decent regimes, power politics are unacceptable, even when dealing with nasty enemies. War should always be defensive, if waged at all. And the decent regimes must help out all other peoples when the need arises.

Illiberal Implications

Rawls's theory of justice suffers from serious weaknesses—so serious that it is not immediately clear why the theory has been so influential. Consider the questionable method Rawls used to derive his two principles. The people in the original position are not real men and women, but ciphers. They affirm Rawls's idea of justice only because they no longer have the ambitions, the attachments, the moral views, the self-awareness, the passions, and the interests that constitute human identity. Real people would not reach the same conclusions because their hopes and interests and beliefs are different—and often clash.

In short, Rawls's is a political philosophy without politics. And as such, it can be troublingly illiberal, replacing the clash of opinion and the necessary trade-offs and compromises of democratic life with what Rawls presents as a purely rational deduction of political morality. Progressive liberalism, it seems, is truth; other political visions are only error.

Nowhere is this illiberal tendency more evident than in *Political Liberalism*'s discussion of abortion. The overlapping consensus the book defends as central to constitutional democracy encompasses only citizens who hold "reasonable" beliefs, Rawls maintains; unreasonable beliefs have no place at the democratic table. But in a short footnote that constitutes *Political Liberalism*'s entire treatment of abortion, Rawls dogmatically defines reasonable in a way that rules out any arguments that deny adult women a right to a first-trimester termination of pregnancy. We can thus sweep away the views of millions of our fellow citizens from public life, Rawls implies, without even bothering to engage them. This is no way to negotiate differences in a liberal democracy, nor to create an overlapping consensus; it is liberal *force majeure*. Extend the same exclusionary tactic to defenders of laissez-faire capitalism or welfare reform—as on Rawlsian grounds one easily could do—and one would find that democracy had shrunk to include only John Rawls and those who agree with him.

This temptation to define his preferred political views as equivalent to rationality itself is present right at the outset in Rawls's original position. Rawls allows behind the veil only those aspects of human psychology he wants his self-interested, rational choosers to have. Why, after all, are those in the original position risk-avoiders rather than risk-takers? Why not take a chance that one might wind up, if not Lebron James, at least a talented overachiever, and endorse institutions that provide maximum opportunity (while still maintaining a safety net, in case one turned out to be Joe Nobody)? From a self-interested standpoint, the risk-taking attitude seems at least as rational as the risk-avoiding one.

A Rawlsian, of course, would point out that the veil supplies the moral constraints within which rational, self-interested choice takes place, and that our intuitions about equality tell us what the veil should obscure. But Rawls simply assumes that we are all egalitarians. He simply assumes that the advantaged recognize that they have no right to the use of their talents and advantages without the permission of an egalitarian society. He simply assumes that justice as fairness will boost social reciprocity and lead to long-term stability. These assumptions ignore both the ambitious drive of the gifted and the corrosive force of envy—two of the most basic human emotions. To be plausible, Rawlsian egalitarianism would need argument, not assumption.

Flight from Reality

Rawls's rationalist, deductive approach also renders his theory extremely abstract. The reader can range over hundreds of pages in Rawls without meeting a historical example or world-historical figure, a comparative analysis of economic or political institutions, a reference to cultural developments, a discussion of crime, an exploration of collective identification (the strongest political force of our age), or anything else connected to the real world. Rawls describes himself as a "realistic utopian." Reality, though, seems to play a limited role in his work.

Rawls discusses "liberal socialism," for example, without once telling us how it might work–an important consideration, one would think, given the many failures of socialism in practice. How would the vast state intervention in the economy and heavy taxation needed to redistribute wealth and opportunities and liberties along Rawlsian lines avoid suppressing entrepreneurial energy and prosperity? Rawls does not say. His emphasis is invariably on the distribution of wealth and other social goods, not on how a society produces them in the first place.

This abstraction mars Rawls's writings on international justice as well. To say that decent societies must only fight defensive wars and must avoid power politics sounds nice, but it ignores the harsh realities of democratic statesmanship, where dirty hands are often unavoidable in protecting liberal citizens against illiberal menaces from abroad (or, as September 11 and the July 2005 London bombings reminded us, from within). For the democratic statesman to pretend otherwise is potentially lethal to those over whose destiny he watches.

This flight from the real is very different from what one finds in political thinkers such as Aristotle or Alexis de Tocqueville or, closer to us in time, Raymond Aron. These theorists do not avoid making moral and political judgments. Yet they show an abiding interest in what history and social theory can tell us about how the world actually works. Rawls detaches moral and political argument from questions of feasibility. The widespread influence of the Rawlsian method has made too much of contemporary political philosophy idle dreaming.

Is It Just?

These are methodological problems in Rawls's thought, but what about justice as fairness itself? Is a conception of justice that "prevents the use of accidents of natural endowment and the contingencies of social circumstances as counters in a quest for political and economic advantage," as Rawls puts it in *A Theory of Justice*, defensible?

The answer must surely be no. To show why, let me borrow a real-world example where something like Rawls's idea of justice is at work. South suburban Chicago, as urban expert Howard Husock notes in the pages of *City Journal*, is home to a number of middle-class black families, many of which have, through hard work and striving, managed to escape the blighted inner city and build better lives in a decent neighborhood. In recent years, though, the federal government has used Section 8 housing vouchers to subsidize ghetto residents to move to south suburban Chicago, in the belief that this nicer, suburban neighborhood will have a positive effect on their life chances. But the new residents have unfortunately brought with them the disorder and crime of the inner city that the hard-working families hoped they had forever left behind. The families that made it to the suburbs through their own efforts, Husock reports, now see those efforts going for naught, and are outraged at what they perceive to be the injustice of the relocation policy.

If Rawls is right, however, these families have no cause to complain. There is nothing in justice as fairness that allows us morally to distinguish the strivers from their dysfunctional Section 8 neighbors, since the economic advantage the strivers have gained is in fact a mere "accident of natural endowment" or a contingency of social circumstance (such as having been raised by loving and involved parents). The inequality that resulted from their ambitions would only be acceptable from a Rawlsian view if it somehow benefited the "worst off." And given that the flight of the strivers has likely made the condition of the inner city worse—their human capital and good example are now lost to their old neighborhood—how has it helped the worst off? The strivers have no right to a nice neighborhood unless everyone else wins too.

There is something profoundly counterintuitive about such a notion of justice. Indeed, it is fundamentally at odds with how most people think about the subject. As one of Rawls's critics, the philosopher John Kekes, explains, "Rawls repudiates the conception—accepted from the Old Testament to recent times—that justice consists in giving people what they deserve: reward for good conduct and punishment for bad." Rawls's idea of justice offers us instead a rather dispiriting world in which individual responsibility and striving have no moral worth. In it, the state ceaselessly shepherds us, redistributing until the end of time, in the hope of diminishing the sting of tragedy and misfortune and bad choices.

There is nobility in the Rawlsian desire to diminish suffering, but great folly as well. Communitarians have rightly criticized Rawls for his excessive individualism—the government neutrality toward different ways of life that Rawls's liberalism requires would indeed result in "the legal disestablishment of morality," in John Gray's evocative phrase, and thus would undermine the cultural prerequisites of a free society. But it is equally plausible to criticize Rawls, as his late Harvard colleague Robert Nozick did in his celebrated *Anarchy, State, and Utopia*, for making the individual the virtual slave of the Nanny State.

Come and Gone?

What accounts for Rawls's remarkable prestige? Three things, I think. First, *A Theory of Justice* appeared at a tumultuous time in American history—progressivism and the New Left had begun their long march through the nation's institutions, and the notion that society as a whole, and not individual behavior, bore the blame for poverty and injustice had become common wisdom among elites. Rawls offered an elaborate theoretical justification for this core belief of the New Left. And as the New Left took over the commanding heights of our society and one wing of the Democratic Party, it has helped keep the spirit of Rawls's thought alive. To see that spirit in action, attend a city council meeting in New York or Oakland when a "living wage" or reparations for black Americans is being debated.

Second, Rawls's theory has provided philosophic cover for liberals who seek to dismiss conservative opinion as rank prejudice. Many liberals deem those on the right immoral or irrational. In his own quiet fashion, Rawls told them they were correct to think this way. In his later writings, Rawls increasingly looked to liberal judges to achieve justice, mirroring the Left's own tendency in recent decades to rely on activist courts to win the battles it could never win at the ballot box.

Then there is a sociological explanation. Rawls's dense writings became a rewarding parlor game for left-wing intellectuals, a game with its own rules and specialized vocabulary. Should the "difference" principle apply to the family? Does Rawls answer Marx's critique of bourgeois rights? Are homosexual rights among the basic liberties? On and on it continues, giving a generation of scholars tenure opportunities. Rawls's entire post–*Theory of Justice* career was caught up in this game, as the notes in his essays and books, which disproportionately refer to articles discussing his work, reveal.

Harvard professor Hillary Putnam, a longtime colleague, claims of Rawls that his work "is not going to be forgotten for decades, I think for centuries." Perhaps. Yet at least on the academic left, his influence may already be waning. Other approaches have begun to take its place—multiculturalism, queer theory, the antiglobalism of Antonio Negri, the soft nihilism of Richard Rorty. Compared with these rivals, Rawls's project, with all its talk of reason and rationality, has come to seem a bit gray and old-fashioned.

7

Bertrand de Jouvenel's Melancholy Liberalism

Compared to other major political thinkers of his generation—including Raymond Aron, Isaiah Berlin, Michael Oakeshott, and Leo Strauss—Bertrand de Jouvenel has suffered from relative neglect. During the 1950s and '60s, this French philosopher and political economist enjoyed a considerable reputation in the English-speaking world. He lectured as a visiting professor at Yale University and the University of California at Berkeley, and his books garnered serious reviews in prestigious journals. But by the time of his death in 1987, his star had dimmed. Read through a span of recent political-theory journals and one will rarely encounter his name.

The neglect is not surprising. Jouvenel's thought does not fit into the two categories that unfortunately came to dominate academic thinking on politics during the 1970s and continue to rule it today: the arid left-liberalism of analytic philosophers like Rawls and Ronald Dworkin, which reduces political thought to abstract reflection on moral and legal principles, and the nihilist radicalism of poststructuralist thinkers like Negri and Michel Foucault, which irresponsibly seeks to destroy the bourgeois world to clear the way for—well, who knows what?

Jouvenel's work, published over five decades in a series of learned, beautifully written books and essays, is anything but abstract. It harkens back to an older style of political thought (as old as Aristotle, really, but arching over the centuries to include Montesquieu and Tocqueville) that combines moral and political philosophy with painstaking historical and institutional analysis.

His work is also a model of political responsibility. Pierre Manent places Jouvenel in the sober tradition of *liberalisme triste*—melancholy liberalism—whose great representative is Tocqueville and among whose recent exemplars I would include Irving Kristol and Manent himself. These anti-utopians fully acknowledge the basic decency and justness of liberal democratic civilization. But they are also aware of its profound weaknesses—the erosion of moral and spiritual life, the hollowing out of civil society, the growth of an overbearing state, and the "joyless quest for joy," as Leo Strauss once put it, of a society dedicated chiefly to commercial pursuits. The task of *liberalisme triste* is to illuminate the tensions and possibilities of this liberal civilization, in the hope of advising citizens and statesmen how best to cultivate the goods and avoid, or at least moderate, the attendant evils.

Thankfully, there are signs that Jouvenel is sparking renewed interest. Over the last decade, two publishers—Liberty Fund Press and Transaction Publishers—have made some of his most important work available again to English readers, and Daniel J. Mahoney published in 2005 a short but luminous book on his thought. It is time, then, to reconsider Jouvenel's contribution to the political theory of democratic capitalism.

A Life in the Age of Extremes

Bertrand de Jouvenel was born in 1903 into an aristocratic French household swept up in the political and intellectual currents of the early twentieth century. His father, Baron Henri de Jouvenel, was a well-known Dreyfusard politician and newspaper editor, and his mother, Sarah Claire Boas, the daughter of a wealthy Jewish industrialist, ran a trendy Parisian salon, which allowed young Bertrand to meet many of the leading artists, writers, and politicians of the day. Through his mother, a passionate supporter of Czechoslovak independence, he gained his earliest political experience, working as private secretary to Eduard Beneš, Czechoslovakia's first prime minister, when barely out of his teens.

Jouvenel was close to both of his parents, who divorced in 1912, but his relationship to his father was sorely tested during the early twenties. After divorcing Bertrand's mother, Henri had married the novelist and sexual provocateur Colette. In 1919, the sixteen-year-old Bertrand, strikingly handsome—"all sinews and lank," observes Colette biographer Judith Thurman—entered a scandalous affair with his stepmother, then in her late forties, who had seduced the bookish teenager. In October 1923, according to one version of events, Henri surprised Bertrand and Colette in bed, definitively ending a marriage that had already soured. A remorseful Bertrand "was horrified to see myself, or to believe myself, the cause of this drama." Still, he continued the affair for two more years. He later patched things up with his father, but Colette always haunted him. Even as an old man, happily married to his second wife Helene (he had briefly married war correspondent Martha Gellhorn during the early 1930s), Jouvenel had difficulty speaking of his forbidden romance without emotion.

Jouvenel's formal education was more conventional than his love life. Subsequent to studying at the Lycee Hoche in Versailles, he graduated from the Sorbonne, where he read in law and mathematics. He later took up a succession of short-term academic posts that culminated in an appointment to the prestigious École Science Politique in 1975. He always regretted not having a steadier academic career, which would have given him the opportunity to mold a generation of students in the manner of Aron and Strauss. However, as founder and director of the think tank SEDEIS (Societé d'Étude et de Documentation Économique, Industrielle, et Sociale), an institution with many connections both inside and outside the academy, he did have a huge impact on the education of French elites by familiarizing them, through regular seminars and publications, with Anglo-American economic ideas.

Jouvenel's political education owed less to the academy than to his extensive work as a journalist, specializing in international relations, from the late 1920s until World War II. As political scientists Marc Landy and Dennis Hale observe, "To a degree unparalleled by any other chronicler of the rise of totalitarianism in the 1930s, even Orwell, de Jouvenel witnessed the key events and came to know the key individuals firsthand." Jouvenel interviewed at length Mussolini, Churchill, and, in a 1935 worldwide exclusive, Hitler. His journalistic activities brought him to various European hotspots, including Austria during the Anschluss and Czechoslovakia during the Nazi invasion. This hands-on experience, note Landy and Hale, gave Jouvenel a feel for the stuff of politics, its tragic contingencies and mundane complexities, its resistance to abstract categories and utopian schemes, its dangers and decencies.

Like many of his generation, Jouvenel became a proponent of liberal democracy only gradually. At the age of twenty-three, he stood unsuccessfully for parliament as a Radical-Socialist candidate. For a while, disgusted by the decadence of the French Third Republic, he sought solace in the other extreme of the political spectrum; in 1936, he joined Jacques Doriot's Parti Populaire Français, a right-wing populist—some would say quasifascist—party. He would leave the party two years later, however, because of Doriot's shameful support for the Munich Pact. His eyes now opened, Jouvenel signed up with the French army intelligence to struggle against the rising Nazi menace. In 1942, following France's armistice with Germany, he worked for the French Resistance, eventually fleeing to Switzerland with the Gestapo in pursuit. By that time, he had become the full-fledged antitotalitarian liberal that he remained the rest of his life.

Jouvenel's flirtation with the radical Right during the thirties came back to trouble him fifty years later, when the Israeli scholar Zeev Sternhell falsely accused him of collaborating with the Nazis. Jouvenel sued for libel in 1983 and won. Raymond Aron, who had left his hospital bed against his doctor's wishes to testify on Jouvenel's behalf, dropped dead of a stroke immediately after telling the court that his longtime friend was "one of the two or three leading political thinkers of his generation"—and no collaborator.

In addition to his journalistic activities, Jouvenel published several books prior to the war, including, in 1928, *L'economie dirigee* (coining the term the French still use for economic planning), a 1933 study of the Great Depression in the United States, and three novels. After the war, he mostly abandoned journalism to concentrate on writing the treatises in political philosophy that won him widespread acclaim. Jouvenel's postwar works contain the three main themes of his mature thought: an effort to understand the hypertrophy of the modern state; a meditation on the common good in pluralistic modern societies; and an attempt to describe the dynamics of political life. Let us look at each in turn.

Beware the Minotaur

Jouvenel wrote his first major work of political philosophy, *On Power: The Natural History of Its Growth*, from Swiss exile as World War II raged and Europe lay in ruins. Its basic aim, one which runs through all of Jouvenel's postwar writings, is to examine how the modern state became so dangerous to human liberty.

The long shadow of the totalitarian state darkens every page of *On Power*. National Socialism and communism, in their quests to revolutionize the bourgeois economic and political condition, had desolated entire nations. Never before had such state power been unleashed. But even in contemporary liberal democratic societies, the centralized state had grown to a disturbing size. Jouvenel's libertarian ideal—"the recognition, or the assumption, that there is in every man the same pride and dignity as had hitherto been assured and protected, but for the aristocracy only, by privileges"—found little breathing room in the collectivist modern world.

Jouvenel's labyrinthine book is a kind of pathology of modern politics. Jouvenel reviews Western history to determine exactly when centralized authority—Power, or the Minotaur, as he alternately calls it—first extended its reach and what allowed it to do so. The Minotaur started to stir, he discovers, in the twelfth century; it grew "continuously" until the eighteenth and has exponentially increased in size since then.

Jouvenel blames Power's growth on several permanent features of centralized government (following Jouvenel, I will capitalize the "p" in "power" whenever referring to the state apparatus). First, the central governing authority naturally seeks dominance. After all, flawed human beings occupy the offices of Power, and they often want to lord over everybody else. "Is not the will to Power rooted deep in human nature?" Jouvenel asks. The desire for dominion is not the whole story of human nature, as Jouvenel would readily agree, but every truthful account of political life—from the biblical narrative of David to George Orwell's *Homage to Catalonia*—recognizes its eternal existence.

The second explanation for the concentration of Power is political rivalry. For political communities to survive military challenge, their leaders must be able to act decisively and forcefully. Fail to match your rival's punch—his capacity swiftly to mobilize his citizenry and levy their wealth or develop deadly new technologies—and you could quickly find yourself out for the count. To keep pace with powerful Spain in the sixteenth and seventeenth centuries, for example, the dynasties of England and France had to take more authority into their hands, increasing the number of men under arms and raising taxes. More recently, during World War II, the allied democracies used propaganda and state direction of the economy—Power-boosting tools generally shunned by free societies—to resist the Nazi war machine. Competition for military supremacy feeds the Minotaur.

The Medieval Moment

These two explanations, true as far as they go, still do not explain why Power started to expand when it did nor why that expansion intensified dramatically after the seventeenth century. To understand that, Jouvenel shows, greater attention to the logic of Western history is necessary. *On Power* exemplifies one of the great virtues of Jouvenel's political thought: in order to expand our perspective on the events affecting us, it shifts our attention from the immediacy of the present, which can be blind, to the past and, as we will see, to the future. In this book, Jouvenel breaks with the popular Enlightenment story—"pure fantasy," he deems it—of monarchs "to whose exactions there are no bounds" and modern democratic governments "whose resources are proportionate to their authority." The true picture, we learn from history, is much more ambiguous.

Consider the Middle Ages. Far from possessing the right to crush men with arbitrary force, the medieval king inhabited a spiritual, moral, and institutional world that bound him tightly. The divine law, as the Catholic Church taught it, limited the king's authority, indeed all human authority, from above. The king was God's servant, with a sacred duty to preserve God's created order. That hierarchical order, among other things, made the king not master of, but simply first among, nobles—each a rival authority with land and forces of his own. To get anything done the king had to go, hat in hand, to his fellow nobles to beg for men and funds, all the while making sure that the church did not disapprove too strongly. In turn, the common law, a human artifact written within the framework of the divine law and borrowing some of its luster, limited Power from below with innumerable precedents and customs. Jouvenel remarks, "The consecrated king of the Middle Ages was a Power as tied down and as little arbitrary as we can conceive." God was sovereign, not men; there was no absolute or uncontrolled human authority.

Some might accuse the Catholic Jouvenel of romanticizing medieval life. I think this is to mistake his point. Of course, kings often rudely violated the law, as Jouvenel admits, and the medieval mindset failed to extend to every man and woman full recognition of the dignity that is their due. But the law wove a religious and customary web around Power that prevented it from completely breaking loose and becoming absolute. Recall, Jouvenel says, that the Catholic Church's sanctions "brought the Emperor Henry IV to fall on his knees before Gregory VII in the snow of Canossa." In such a universe, Power could expand only slowly.

This complex web began to unravel when European kings, keen to boost their authority, threw their lot in with the people to defeat the nobles who had kept Power in check. The people looked to the kings to free them from the petty and sometimes not-so-petty oppressions of the aristocrats, whom the kings, in top Machiavellian form, had successfully encouraged to ditch their age-old responsibilities to the plebs. From this alliance between kings and the masses arose, beginning in the fifteenth century and lasting until the eighteenth, Europe's absolute monarchies. These absolute monarchs, no longer checked by rival aristocrats, centralized and modernized Power and wielded resources far greater than had medieval kings. The Protestant Reformation also helped destroy the medieval order and amplify monarchical Power by giving reformed princes leeway to redefine the meaning of divine laws and to disregard custom; Catholic princes, to keep up, began to skirt the church's rules themselves. The Minotaur grew.

Democracy on Trial

But what really triggered Power's dramatic expansion, Jouvenel suggests, was the birth of the democratic age, which finished off what was left of the dying medieval order. The political scientist Pierre Hassner, a keen reader of Jouvenel, elaborates: *On Power* "is a generalization of Alexis de Tocqueville's idea that the French Revolution, rather than breaking the absolutism of the state, further concentrated power in the hands of the state." Jouvenel sees the democratic era as extending Power's reach in at least three different but related ways.

First and most fundamental is the triumph in the eighteenth century of the doctrine of popular sovereignty, the idea that "the people," not some divine source or ancient custom, have final authority on all matters of law and social organization. "The denial of a divine lawgiving and the establishment of a human lawgiving," warns Jouvenel, "are the most prodigious strides which a society can take towards a truly absolute Power." Outside of small communities, popular sovereignty, taken literally, is absurd. The people themselves cannot actually govern, and so pretty soon others—often a single other—rule in their name. These new rulers find it easier than ever to direct and mobilize society.

Popular sovereignty erodes the restraints on what political communities can imagine doing. If the law is solely an expression of the people's will, where would the limits on it come from? Anything becomes possible: the rounding up of political opponents, the bombing of civilians, laws condemning minorities or the unfit to extinction, the creation of genetic monstrosities or supermen.

In addition, popular sovereignty encourages the notion that the state is a tool for directly securing the people's wellbeing. Power is accordingly burdened with a surfeit of new responsibilities, from running jobs programs and providing welfare, to redistributing wealth and regulating businesses, to funding scientific research and guaranteeing education to all citizens. Whether or not such activities are reasonable and salutary, they act to increase the reach of the state.

Popular sovereignty also brings mass conscription: since everyone ostensibly has an equal stake in Power, everyone must defend it. The historian Hippolyte Taine put it well: universal suffrage and mass conscription are like "twin brothers . . . the one placing in the hands of every adult person a voting paper, the other putting on his back a soldier's knapsack." The "Sun King," Louis XIV, the most absolute of absolute monarchs, would have loved to institute conscription for his endless wars across seventeenth-century Europe, but he felt himself powerless to do it. It was the French Revolution that first militarized the masses and sent them forth across Europe's battlefields.

The second way in which the democratic age extended Power was through the unleashing of relativism. Popular sovereignty was interpreted to mean self-sovereignty, the right of each individual to decide his own right and wrong. This Protagorism, as Jouvenel terms it, in which man becomes the measure of all things, summons the Minotaur to quell the social disorder that is inevitably unleashed. In a later work, he gravely writes, "To the entire extent to which progress develops hedonism and moral relativism, to which individual liberty is conceived as the right of man to obey his appetites, nothing but the strongest of powers can maintain society in being."

Jouvenel pointed out that relativism calls forth Power a second way. The loss of objective standards is existentially unbearable, opening "an aching void in the room of beliefs and principles." The secular religions of communism and National Socialism drew nourishment from this crisis of meaning, building up Power to truly monstrous proportions. In Jouvenel's stark account, totalitarianism is born of the modern world's moral confusion.

Finally, Power grows in the democratic age because of the erosion of civil society. Democratic regimes base themselves on the individual, and individualism tends to hollow out or even utterly destroy civil society. The modern state wages a relentless attack on "social authorities"—in today's policy jargon, the mediating structures of families, churches, businesses, and other associations that stand between the state and the individual and constitute extra-individual sources of authority and meaning. The attack can he blunt and brutal, as in the totalitarian regimes' total repression of civil society. Or it can take a softer form, as when the bureaucratic and inefficient welfare state usurps from families the responsibility for rearing children. In either case, though on very different scales, one finds state Power vastly increased and individual liberties menaced or obliterated. In a social field in which there are but two actors—Power and the individual—humans cannot flourish.

Jouvenel does not have much good to say about the liberal democratic West in *On Power*. He does suggest that the flickering light of political and human liberty might be sustained by supporting moral and religious belief in a "higher code" that restrains human willfulness, and by educating leaders and citizens to be vigilant of Power, like their medieval predecessors. But he views the separation-of-powers doctrine advocated by eighteenth- and nineteenth-century liberal constitutionalists as a weak reed against Power's tank-like advance. Since all modern constitutions base themselves on the people's will, they will not long deter Power's advance.

In fact, Jouvenel's argument in *On Power* risks becoming a kind of reverse Marxism, in which history ends not in bliss but in the concentration camp. The gigantic state is "the culmination of the history of the West," he observes in the book's grim closing paragraphs, implying that we cannot do much about it. Thankfully, the evolution of the democracies in the years since Jouvenel wrote the book does not bear out his gloomiest warnings.

Despite its excessive pessimism, *On Power* stands as a permanent warning to liberal democratic regimes that their freedom is difficult to sustain, for reasons inseparable from the logic of their own principles. And in Jouvenel's ensuing work, most evocatively in *Sovereignty: An Inquiry into the Political Good*, he develops a more constructive political science, one which looks more positively upon liberal constitutionalism.

Between Thick and Thin

Published in 1957, *Sovereignty* is Jouvenel's masterpiece and one of the great works in the tradition of *liberalisme triste*. Along with revisiting *On Power*'s concerns about the dangers of popular sovereignty, it explores what the earlier book left unexamined. If collectivism is not the inevitable destiny of modern liberal democratic societies, then how best might they avoid it? What kind of excellences might liberal democracies achieve? In *Sovereignty* and other writings from the fifties and sixties, Jouvenel offers a dynamic and political conception of the common good that reinforces the best virtues and combats the worst vices of liberal regimes.

On Power might give the impression that Jouvenel is a partisan of the ancien régime or even the classical polis, but his postwar writings make clear that he only has one foot planted in the old world. Jouvenel, like Aristotle before him, believes that there is such a thing as the political good, and that it cannot be defined as the sum total of my individual good plus your individual good plus everybody else's individual good. Man is not just a selfish animal but also a social and political animal, for whom certain essential goods exist only because he belongs to a political community.

However, this idea of the political good does not require an attempt to restore the ancient polis. Down that road, Jouvenel argues, lies tragedy. To use state power to try to bring back the closed community and moral harmony of the classical city in a pluralistic modern liberal society would be utopian. It would involve massive coercion and still ultimately prove unsuccessful, as all such efforts since the French Revolution have shown, with grave consequences.

There is a simple reason such projects bring tyranny: The world has changed since the time of Pericles. Four "corollaries" that were preconditions for the "thick" community of the ancient city no longer apply today. The first is small size. "The city must not become too large," Jouvenel observes, "for otherwise, when the number of citizens is too great for intimacy between them to be possible, the harmony is less intense." How small? Plato claims roughly 5,000 families—like a small American town. Next is complete homogeneity. Even the inhabitants of a small town in America would not match the uniformity of culture and educational background of a classical Greek city. Yet without homogeneity of this sort, the harmony of the classical polis is impossible. The third and fourth corollaries also concern maintaining harmony. The third: "It is dangerous to allow the entry into the city of beliefs and customs from outside, for these create a motley variety of reactions and practices." So, no immigration, no CNN, no foreign literature, no travel outside the city's walls. Corollary four is immutability. The community must snuff out the fire of innovation everywhere it threatens to blaze up.

One begins to get the picture. The polis is oppressive—perhaps even suffocating. Exactly what characterizes liberal democratic modernity—"the enlargement of societies, the aggregation of disparate peoples, the contagion of cultures, and the burgeoning of novelties," in Jouvenel's words—is what the corollaries definitively rule out. Yet most of us do see important goods in big cities: the free clash of ideas and sensibilities and beliefs, contact with foreign cultures, and fancy new toys like high-definition televisions, to say nothing about new medicines to treat disease. To try to impose some blueprint of the common good that would regulate this complex, open reality would of necessity be tyrannical.

The upshot: the classical goods of complete harmony and thick community that the modern world has undermined—and there is no doubt that they are goods—are incompatible with other goods that we cannot imagine living without. Too many armchair communitarians, on the left and the right, simply fail to see this.

If Jouvenel rejects a metaphorical return to Greece as destructive of our modern freedoms, however, he stops short of the libertarianism that, say, Charles Murray argues for in *What It Means to Be a Libertarian.* In Murray's view, government should do next to nothing. It ought to refuse to make judgments about citizens' moral choices, instead giving the market and the institutions of civil society free reign and intervening only when monopolists or thieves or murderers mess things up.

This thin understanding of the political, Jouvenel contends, is not an adequate governing philosophy for a modern liberal democracy. Indeed, to the extent that government, basing itself on the self-sovereignty of man, refuses to discriminate between moral and immoral choices, it surrenders to the relativism that already troubles liberal societies. As *On Power* shows, such relativism beckons the state to restore the order it destroys and to fill the spiritual emptiness it creates.

For Jouvenel, the modern democratic state has a much more extensive moral task: to create the conditions that let "social friendship"—a common good compatible with the goods and freedoms of modernity—blossom. Jouvenel describes this modern common good as resting "in the strength

121

of the social tie, the warmth of the friendship felt by one citizen for another and the assurance each has of predictability in another's conduct." To nurture this mutual trust is the essence of the art of politics.

Jouvenel scholars Mahoney and David DesRosiers, in their illuminating introduction to *Sovereignty*, correctly observe that the book "contains one of the richest accounts of the permanent requirements of statesmanship written in this [the twentieth] century." Among the tasks of the liberal statesman are the following (this is by no means an exhaustive list). First, the statesman must prudentially balance innovation and conservation. Modern societies, severed from the past, are open, mobile, and constantly transforming. Government needs to respond to this constant flux with policies that attenuate some of its worst effects. A world that is always changing is, as noted earlier, for many human beings profoundly alienating. Thus, Jouvenel would be willing, for example, to use government funds to retrain workers displaced by a new technology.

One way of pursuing this balance is to anticipate future trends as much as possible in order to cushion their impact. Hence Jouvenel's extensive research in "future studies," given its fullest theoretical treatment in a fascinating but sadly out-of-print 1968 book titled *The Art of Conjecture,* in which Jouvenel again challenges what I would call our presentism. The "art" in the title is a tip-off. In Jouvenel's view, there is no science of the future, only reasoned inferences from existing trends.

Another task of the statesman is to do nothing to harm and everything possible to help a culture of ordered liberty prosper, short of imposing a state truth. As we have seen, the free society cannot survive if license prevails. At a minimum, this means a statesman should be a model of self-restraint in his own life. But one can imagine an array of policies that would shore up, rather than weaken, ordered liberty without resorting to massive state coercion. Of course, the political leader cannot do this alone. This is a task for all citizens of a free society, particularly those who participate in culture-forming institutions.

The statesman must also regulate "noxious activities" that threaten social friendship. In a Jouvenelian liberal democracy, racists would get no license to march. Parties that advocated revolution or violence would find no home, either. Jouvenel believes that civility is crucial to a free society.

And finally, the statesman must deflate hopes for a permanent solution to the political problem. There is no ultimate solution in politics, only temporary "settlements," as Jouvenel put it in a later book. To try to conjure up ancient Greece again or to dispense with politics altogether (the communitarian and libertarian dreams, respectively) are both solutions, not settlements. Politics is our permanent this-worldly condition; to deny that fact is to create, or at least tempt, tyranny.

The Good and Bad of Capitalism

Nowhere is there greater need for vigilance in cultivating the common good in modern democracies than with regard to the free market. Jouvenel is a strong defender of the efficiency and productivity of a free economy. The capitalist dynamo has eased life for millions, giving them choices and opportunities and time unavailable to all but the few in pre-modern societies. Jouvenel knows that economic growth and consumer satisfaction are the imperatives that drive our societies.

But having more goodies does not in itself constitute the good life. Like Pope Benedict XVI, Jouvenel argues that a strong moral culture and vigorous political institutions must serve as makeweights against the market. Thus, Jouvenel would probably have had few qualms about cracking down on Hollywood violence and fashion-industry kiddie-porn ads. For just as government has a responsibility to educate citizens politically, so too it is important to lift the preferences of consumers to higher ends. "We live in majority societies where beautiful things will be wiped out unless the majority appreciates them," Jouvenel observed during the sixties. A market society is praiseworthy only if the choices people make within it are praiseworthy.

Another area in which the market needs public oversight is the environment. In a highly organized modern society, Jouvenel wrote in the 1957 essay "From Political Economy to Political Ecology," "Nature disappears behind the mass of our fellow creatures." We forget what we owe it. I can imagine some conservative readers rushing to put Jouvenel back on the shelf at this point. But Jouvenel's green thumb is much closer to regulatory theorist Peter Huber's (or Theodore Roosevelt's) market-friendly conservationism than it is to Arne Naess's antihumanist deep ecology.

The environment is for man, not man for the environment—that biblical insight is one Jouvenel embraces. Modern economies have made man master of the earth, and that is potentially to the good, he says. But with mastery comes responsibility. In a 1968 essay titled "The Stewardship of the Earth," Jouvenel sums up his environmental vision: "The Earth has been given to us for our utility and enjoyment, but also entrusted to our care, that we should be its caretakers and gardeners." This is sensible stuff. It means smart environmental regulations to establish wildlife reserves, clean up rivers, protect endangered species, and punish toxic dumpers, not trying to restore some preindustrial arcadia (there's that anti-utopianism again).

If Jouvenel's support for the free market stops short of an idolatry of choice and the right to pollute, it enthusiastically resists government interventions aimed at redistributing wealth. "Only Hayek has rivaled Bertrand de Jouvenel in demonstrating why redistributionism in the democracies results in the atrophy of personal responsibility and the hypertrophy of the bureaucracy and the centralized state instead of in relief to the hapless minorities it is pledged to serve," says Robert Nisbet about a book Jouvenel published in 1952 called *The Ethics of Redistribution.* In this short, profound study, Jouvenel ignores (though he agrees with it) the economic argument against the redistribution of wealth: that it eats away at incentives and so impoverishes everyone. Instead, he concentrates on the moral arguments against redistribution in an indictment of contemporary left-liberalism as damning as we have.

Jouvenel's three arguments remain unanswered. One is that redistribution quickly becomes regressive. Jouvenel shows that levying the wealth of the rich does not provide nearly enough economic resources to offer a subsistence minimum to the down-and-out. Instead, government must dip into the pockets of the middle class and even the lower-middle class, who themselves receive income transfers. This insight, avers Jouvenel, upsets the widely held belief "that our societies are extremely rich and that their wealth is merely maldistributed." Pursuing redistribution in the face of this truth, he adds, "involves the debasement of even the lower middle-class standard of life." Society becomes proletarianized.

The second argument against redistribution is that it corrodes personal responsibility. By providing for basic needs, the redistributionist state weakens the individual's independence and civil society's authority, threatening to make people into dependent drones. This also reinforces the modern impulse toward centralization described in *On Power.*

Finally, redistribution, by confiscating higher incomes, means that the wealthy must curtail their support of life's amenities: the more redistribution there is, the fewer grants to symphonies, museums, university endowments, parks, and so on. If these amenities are to continue to exist, the state must fund them directly, and it will invariably use a utilitarian calculus in deciding what to fund. One gray vision starts to prevail, not a thousand, or hundreds of thousands, of varied visions. Jouvenel implies that a bourgeois society is much more likely to support high culture than is a redistributionist state.

Jouvenel knew that the impulse to shake down the rich and give to the poor is a permanent temptation in democratic capitalist regimes. There will always be calls from those whom the market has not benefited to redress their plight through politics; and there will always be politicians ready to court their votes. Redistributionism is unlikely ever to disappear in modern societies, but we can try to limit its scope.

A Real Science of Politics

Jouvenel's final contribution to the study of politics is a detailed analysis of its workings, not as a replacement for reflection on the good (as undertaken in *Sovereignty*) but as a supplement to it. The hope is to make political science useful to the statesman, who, as we have seen, has a responsibility to cultivate the social friendship and civility that vivifies the free society and slows the Minotaur's advance. Jouvenel's most comprehensive effort in this vein is a difficult, chiseled book first published in 1963 and recently reissued, *The Pure Theory of Politics.*

This book focuses not on political statics (the juridical forms of constitutions and institutions) but on political dynamics: the phenomenon of "man moving man." One source of political influence is what Cicero called *potestas*: the authority that inheres in someone because of his institutional position. The U.S. military brass may not have liked the idea of draft-dodging ex-hippie Bill Clinton being their commander-in-chief, but their respect for the *potestas* of the presidency meant that they jumped when he said jump. The other source is *potentia*: the kind of authority that is based on the raw ability to get men to do your bidding and to follow your lead. It is the influence of an effective basketball coach or teacher, or, more importantly for Jouvenel's purpose, of the charismatic politician. It is as natural as rain.

Potentia can be a good thing in politics. Churchill's heroic rallying of the English people during World War II would have been unthinkable if he did not possess *potentia*. It can also be dangerously irrational, tapping into forces that can sweep up entire populations in grand passions. How else to describe Hitler's Mephistophelean influence over the Germans? "It is profoundly unsafe to assume that people act rationally in politics," as Jouvenel somberly notes.

The ostensible aim of *The Pure Theory of Politics* is description. Jouvenel intended the book primarily for an audience of American social scientists, nearly all of whom thought that the study of political life should be as free of values as the study of physics. Yet the book is a subtle critique of their abstract social science. Dry academicians said they looked at behavior, but what they meant were things like voting patterns, not strong behavior, behavior of the kind that Machiavelli chronicles with such lucidity.

Thus, the real purpose of *The Pure Theory of Politics* is to remind liberal democrats, who often betray an unwarranted faith in human reasonableness, that politics is not always, or even often, guided by the light of reason; it is often messy, sinister, mad, and tragic, as Thucydides and Shakespeare—Jouvenel's chosen guides in this odd but beautiful book—show us. Were they chastened by this lesson, today's leaders might appreciate the fragility of liberal communities and strive to create the conditions for the growth of social friendship.

Bertrand de Jouvenel's melancholy liberalism has a lot to teach us, though for those who like their politics sunny-side-up it does not come as good news. Jouvenel reassures us that liberal democracies can attain true human goods, including meaningful freedom, social friendship, and widespread prosperity. But these fragile societies must remain on guard, lest their many weaknesses overwhelm their undeniable strengths.

8

The Absolute Intellectual

Back in the 1960s, or even early '70s, if you asked the average intelligent person to name a philosopher, the answer would as likely have been Jean-Paul Sartre as it would have been Aristotle or Plato. "The Pope of Existentialism," as people called him, enjoyed household-name status. By the time of his death in 1980, however, Sartre's fame had already diminished. The 50,000 mourners who shuffled after his casket to Montparnasse cemetery in Paris represented a last flare from his vanishing celebrity, not a sign of real influence. Structuralism, poststructuralism, feminism, colonial studies—as new radical enthusiasms swept through Paris and through the Western academy, existentialism came for many to seem a mere footnote in the history of twentieth-century thought. Who still took seriously *The Critique of Dialectical Reason* or even *Being and Nothingness* and *Nausea*?

For Bernard-Henri Lévy, contemporary France's leading public intellectual and a major media star, this neglect of Sartre's thought and literature is a significant mistake. In fact, he argues in *Sartre: The Philosopher of the Twentieth Century* (first published to acclaim in France in 2000, and in English three years later in a translation by Andrew Brown), Sartre's work is "the meeting point of all the ways of getting through the twentieth century, getting lost in it, avoiding its dark and slippery slopes—and all the ways of setting it off, now, into the new century." Plunging into that work once again, Lévy claims, will help protect us against future threats to human liberty. Lévy's thick book—a kind of intellectual biography-*cum*-philosophical meditation—vigorously defends the man he calls "the absolute intellectual."

Lévy is right about the need to read Sartre, but his admiration is misplaced. What Sartre actually offers us is a paradigmatic example of the leftist mind, in all its dodgy enthusiasms. Sartre's early existentialism presents a nihilistic conception of human freedom that still informs some forms of liberal thought; his later political writings seethe with the pathologies of the far Left, including an admiration for bloodletting, so long as it targets democrats, capitalists, and Westerners generally. Sartre may indeed have been "the absolute intellectual," but only in a negative sense: His oeuvre stands as an absolute warning about the wrong turns that moral and political thought can take when untethered from nature or any sense of reality. Were Sartre alive today, he doubtless would place the blame for September 11 and Palestinian suicide bombings on their victims—defending, as he frequently did, the indefensible.

Sartre's Early Career

Jean-Paul Sartre was born in Paris in June 1905 into a bourgeois family. His mother, born Anne Marie Schweitzer, was a relative of the Christian missionary, theologian, and musician Albert Schweitzer; his father, Jean-Baptiste, was a military officer who died in 1906. After Jean-Baptiste's death, Sartre's mother returned to live with the Schweitzers. Her father, Charles, became Sartre's nominal *père*. In his 1963 autobiography *Words,* Sartre described his childhood as introverted and lonely, blaming Charles Schweitzer for keeping him away from other kids—though he never lacked for love.

Revealingly, *Words* ends at Sartre's twelfth year, when his mother remarried an engineer, Joseph Mancy. Sartre revered his mother, and Lévy—rightly, I believe—suggests that her remarriage was a trauma from which he never fully recovered. Sartre and his followers would later toss around the word "engineer" as a term of ultimate opprobrium. When Mancy later died, Sartre took in his mother, and they shared an apartment for much of his adult life.

Sartre may have been a lonely mama's boy, but he dazzled academically and won entry in 1924 to the École Normale Supérieure, France's premier institute of higher learning for literature and philosophy. Ironically, in 1928 he failed the *Agrégation de philosophie* needed for a teaching career. He took the test again the next year, however, and finished first, just ahead of Simone de Beauvoir, the "Beaver," who became his intellectual companion and lifelong lover and partner (though a far from exclusive one). Soon he was teaching in Le Havre, an unfashionable French seaport. He longed for attention and Paris cafe life, but he still had to wait.

Sartre's writing career took off with the publication in 1938 of his disturbing novel *Nausea,* followed the next year by a collection of short stories, *The Wall,* and in 1943 by the massive philosophical treatise *Being and Nothingness.* During this period of surging productivity, which also included writing for the theater, Sartre did a stint in the French military (in a noncombat meteorological section, due to near blindness in his left eye), spent a year or so as a German prisoner of war following the swift French defeat, and, after his release in August 1941 (the Nazis regarded him as a harmless civilian), returned to occupied Paris, where he taught philosophy at the Lycée Condorcet.

From his nestled corner of the Café Flore—where, when not teaching, he could usually be found drinking tea and scribbling furiously—Sartre did next to nothing for the Resistance while watching his writings win acclaim and his plays enjoy throngs of admirers.

He never actively collaborated with the German occupation authorities—Lévy defends him convincingly on that score—but his relatively cushy wartime experience did later draw the ire of writer and Gaullist minister André Malraux. "I was facing the Gestapo," grumbled Malraux, "while Sartre in Paris had his plays produced with the authorization of the German censors."

The Shock of Existentialism

It is the writing of this early Sartre that Lévy so esteems, calling it "a shock, an event, a tremor, torrent, a tidal wave." The worldview that runs through all of Sartre's work of this period, soon dubbed "existentialism," based itself on several key themes.

The first was the purported Death of God and the meaninglessness of existence. Sartre's protagonist in the hallucinatory *Nausea*, Antoine Roquentin, laments the "total gratuity and absurd contingency of the universe." "Every existing thing is born without reason, prolongs itself out of weakness, and dies by chance," Roquentin says, struggling against a powerful urge to vomit. Lévy sums up this bleak Sartrean vision of man adrift: "Life has no meaning. . . . No promise dwells in it. No invisible hand is guiding it in secret. It is chaotic. Shapeless. Pure disorder and fog. A tangle of moments in disarray. Chaos. A mess."

Roquentin overcomes his dread and disgust only by recognizing what he deems to be the liberating possibilities for the individual consciousness of a contingent universe. "All is free," he resolves: We can create our own meanings, our own ethics, our own futures, our own multiplicity of selves. Roquentin meditates on an American jazz song he loves— "Some of These Days"—and imagines a musician in a New York apartment finding his reason for living in composing it. "Why not me?" he then asks himself, and concludes that he, too, will create something to triumph over contingency: He will write a novel.

Man's freedom of will—another central theme of the early Sartre—is what makes such creative acts possible. Drawing on German and French philosophical sources—Martin Heidegger, Friedrich Nietzsche, and Henri Bergson, among others—Sartre explained that human beings, unlike, say, oak trees and snakes, choose their own future, even when, trapped in "bad faith," they pretend they do not. Man has no nature that predetermines what he will eventually become. His *existence* precedes his *essence*, as the Sartrean formulation puts it.

One problem this choosing self runs up against is how to regard *other* choosing selves. A third existentialist motif, best summed up in Sartre's famous phrase "Hell is other people," shows how Sartre understood that problem. Few writers have ever offered a nastier depiction of human interaction, as Lévy underscores: "[Sartre] cannot imagine any encounter between consciousnesses which does not immediately and definitively turn into a bout of fisticuffs." Friendship? Just mutual exploitation. Love? Simply what Sartre calls pursuing "the death of the Other." Sex? Always a kind of violence, at least in part.

Lévy finds in the thinking of this "first Sartre" a potent weapon against utopianism—and hence against the totalitarian temptation. That is a stretch, to say the least. If the universe is pointless and morals and values simply something we make up as we go along—hypotheses asserted by Sartre but never proven—then why should one free choice matter more than another? The life of an evil brute becomes as praiseworthy as a life dedicated to alleviating suffering.

More: Why should freedom itself matter, if Sartre is right? Why not surrender our will to the mob? The existentialist has no principled answers to such questions—any more than do relativistic contemporary liberals, who share the Sartrean belief that we make up our own values. Sartre the existentialist is in one sense the unacknowledged intellectual father of Richard Rorty, who also believes that contingency goes "all the way down."

As for Sartre's description of human interaction as a war of egos, it expands what is worst within men and women into the overriding law of life. It fails to capture the love we have for our children and spouses or to do justice to the real friendships we forge with others and the commitments we make to church and country and shared projects. The agonistic world Sartre depicts is—precisely from an existential point of view—"unbearable and unlivable," to quote again the apt formulation of Rocco Buttiglione. It is significant, I think, that Sartre never married or committed himself exclusively to Beauvoir, that he disliked children and sired none of his own, that he regularly broke off friendships, and that in general he spent most of his time worshiping at his own altar. He was—to use his own language—a bit of a "bastard." But even the father of atheist existentialism could be generous with the wealth his books' sales and commissions brought him, often using that wealth to help friends. Even he launched shared projects, including the magazine *Les Temps Modernes*, still going strong today, more than a half-century after the debut of its first issue.

Loving Tyranny

After the war, Sartre, now a celebrity, grew radically politicized. He turned into something of a Marxist—an engagé intellectual. Lévy describes how Sartre's year as a prisoner of war, where he "swooned with pleasure" amid the muck and degradation of camp life, rubbing shoulders with unvarnished "humanity," led him to embrace the communitarian—and ultimately totalitarian—politics that characterized his postwar work. But Lévy never explains why, if Sartre's early libertarian thought supposedly inoculates us against totalitarianism, the absolute intellectual could so easily become one of Marxist totalitarianism's most steadfast defenders, a toady for despotism (which led to his famous split with Albert Camus, who had much better sense).

In fact, Sartre's thought provides no such inoculation. His existentially unbearable individualism demands to be overcome. Yet his loathing for prosaic forms of community—*Nausea* depicts bourgeois life as fit only for unthinking cows—encourages a quest for a community on the level of politics. Marx was the answer.

To his credit, Lévy lays out Sartre's ugly postwar record in black and white. It makes for unsettling reading today. Returning in the early fifties from his first visit to the Soviet Union, where Stalinist minders had given the tour, Sartre proclaimed, Walter Duranty–style, that the citizen of the USSR had the "entire freedom to criticize," indeed, that he "criticizes more and in a much more effective manner" than the French worker. He eventually admitted that he knew this was a lie.

In December 1952, in Vienna, at a time of the "darkest repression" in Eastern Europe, Lévy notes, Sartre did a song and dance for the communist bosses at the annual congress of the World Movement for Peace—in other words, the Stalinist International.

Later, Sartre, accompanied by Beauvoir, took a whirlwind tour of Castro's Cuba, led around by the nose by the Generalissimo himself. Upon his return to Paris, Sartre wrote sixteen fawning portraits of Castro—the "man of the whole and the detail." (The French publisher Gallimard has reissued these writings in book form, as if they possessed any kind of truth.)

Justifying his refusal of the Nobel Prize for literature, given to him in 1964, Sartre claimed that the award was a tainted Western prize directed against his Eastern bloc political family—a justification Lévy rightly calls a "gigantic and despicable piece of stupidity." Even as Sartre praised totalitarian dictators, he was describing the United States as "rabid" and Nazi-like, urging France to break off all relations with it. During the Vietnam War, he went so far as to wish for a nuclear strike on America to put an end to its imperialist tendencies. When he criticized the Soviets, as he did after they invaded Hungary in November 1956, he would denounce the bourgeois democracies in the same breath.

Sartre's political writings and public statements now celebrated revolutionary violence. In 1952's *The Communists and Peace*, he raved about communist "mass democracy"—which achieved a unanimity "constantly renewed by the liquidation of opponents." The anticommunist was a "dog," he spat; like many on the left today, Sartre substituted invective for debate. In his well-known preface to Franz Fanon's 1961 anticolonial polemic *The Wretched of the Earth*, Sartre asserted that, for the black man, "to shoot down a European is to kill two birds with one stone, to destroy an oppressor and the man he oppresses at the same time." Historian Paul Johnson later commented: "This was an updating of existentialism: self-liberation through murder."

By the seventies, Sartre had become nothing more than an apologist for tyranny and terror. Though he opposed anti-Semitism and generally supported the Jewish cause, he defended the killing of eleven Israeli athletes by Palestinian terrorists at the 1972 Olympics in Munich. He found it "perfectly scandalous" that "the Munich attack should be judged by the French press and a section of public opinion as an intolerable scandal." Like those who excuse Palestinian homicide bombings today, Sartre held that the only way the Palestinian people could "show its courage and the strength of its hatred" was by "organizing deadly attacks" against civilians. Embracing Maoism, he demanded that capitalist bosses be bled like pigs. "A revolutionary regime must get rid of a certain number of individuals that threaten it and I see no other means for this than death; it is always possible to get out of a prison; the revolutionaries of 1793 probably didn't kill enough people," he said.

The chief theoretical work of this "second" Sartre, *The Critique of Dialectical Reason*, written in a drug-fueled frenzy and first published in 1961, is one of the scariest books to come from the pen of a major twentieth-century thinker. Depicting man as lost in an alienated world of institutions and social exchanges, Sartre maintains that freedom is possible only when men act collectively—and that their unity should be enforced by "Terror." The conservative British political philosopher Maurice Cranston captured Sartre's argument in a succinct formulation (it took Sartre nearly seven hundred pages): "Terror is the guarantee that my neighbor will stay my brother; it binds my neighbor to me by the threat of the violence it will use against him if he dares to be 'unbrotherly.'" Forget such niceties as the rule of law.

Sartre's political thought simply ignored the constraints and possibilities of real political life. The social theorist and conservative liberal Raymond Aron, Sartre's old chum from the École Normale and his great intellectual rival in postwar France, had it exactly right (echoing Tocqueville's charge against the architects of the French Revolution): Sartre was a "literary" political thinker. Sartre preferred, explained Aron, to promote "a literary image of a desirable society, rather than to study the functioning of a given economy, of a liberal economy, of a parliamentary system, and so forth," and he refused ever to ask the question: "if you were in the minister's position, what would you do?" The reader will find no indication in Sartre's thousands of pages of political writings that he had even a rudimentary understanding, say, of political economy or comparative politics.

Nevertheless, faced with the contrast between Sartre's revolutionary fantasies and Aron's prudent wisdom, and despite Sartre's loss of prestige, two generations of the French Left have embraced the dictum that "it is better to be wrong with Sartre than right with Aron."

A Final, Libertarian Sartre?

By the late seventies Sartre had become blind, feeble, and incontinent. He became friends and began to collaborate with a young Jew from Cairo, Benny Lévy, who used the *nom de plume* Peter Victor. Victor's presence incensed the Sartrean camp, especially Beauvoir; they saw him as an interloper who was leading the doddering master astray. Bernard-Henri Lévy, though, believes a third Sartre was emerging, one inspired by Jewish philosopher and ethicist Emmanuel Levinas and with a renewed commitment to freedom. No one will ever know for sure. All that this Sartre left behind, regrets Lévy, is "a phantom oeuvre, forever unrealized."

By the time the reader reaches the end of Lévy's book,

he is left wondering, despite the author's intention, whether there is anything in Sartre worth holding on to, apart from the negative example he offers of a mind adrift. The answer is yes, I think. Sartre's literary innovations—putting novelistic touches in his philosophy and philosophy in his novels—and his ambition to be creative in so many disciplines are admirable. The American writer Walker Percy claimed to have found a model for his richly philosophical novels in Sartre's work, proving that writers who do not share Sartre's politics can use his literary innovations.

Some of Sartre's writings—*Nausea*, his unfinished novel series *The Roads to Freedom*, *Being and Nothingness*, the play *No Exit*—contain real, if exaggerated or distorted, insights into the human condition. Read as descriptions not of a permanent truth of man's fate but of the predicament of a certain kind of modern man, one who has lost his reference points in God and nature and found nothing to replace them, they still resonate.

That said, most of his endless outpouring of words is today unreadable. (Sartre never shut up, as film director John Huston complained when the two worked together on a biopic of Freud and the former handed in a fat screenplay far too long to be of any use.) Whatever small measure of merit it might still contain, Jean-Paul Sartre's work ultimately leaves one to ponder a mystery: how such a brilliant man could be so stupid.

9

Liberal Folly and Conservative Peace

I remember a lecture some years back, when I was in graduate school, that provided one of those rare flashes that illuminate an entire universe. The speaker was a widely published political philosopher (and, as I later discovered, a former Jesuit priest). His topic was typical for the kind of analytic liberal theory that he practiced: how best to interpret, and implement, equality, particularly when faced with modern feminism's demands. For this philosopher, "our intuitions" led us inexorably down a single path, at the end of which, once medical advances made it physically possible, men should give birth to children. Only with such a species mutation—an engineered hermaphroditism—would equality between men and women be possible, gender roles rendered a matter of choice, not destiny.

Much of contemporary liberal political philosophy—the philosophy of John Rawls (see chapter 6), Ronald Dworkin, Thomas Nagel, and their many followers—is captured in this astonishing argument: the denial of any intrinsic dignity to the human world; the reconceptualization of moral life along contractualist lines; the elevation of equality and autonomy above all other goods; the dismissal of philosophical analysis of foundations, metaphysical or otherwise; and, finally, a contempt for what most people believe and have believed for most of history. "Our intuitions," for this liberal philosopher, were the intuitions of liberal academics, not the moral sentiments of a common humanity.

Reading the conservative moral philosopher and Hungarian émigré John Kekes's lucid, careful, and often profound books and essays of the last thirty years—writings exploring the nature of evil, the limits of egalitarianism, the poverty of liberalism, the role of the moral imagination, and the art of living, among many other fertile topics—brought this memory flooding back. For it's exactly the kind of empty theorizing indulged in by the former Jesuit that Kekes's work consistently condemns, and itself avoids.

Liberal Dead Ends

In Kekes's view, contemporary liberal theory is deeply incoherent. The negative goals that liberals pursue can be summarized under the heading of the *avoidance of evil*: liberals wish to protect individuals from "dictatorship, torture, poverty, intolerance, repression, discrimination, lawlessness," and other affronts to human dignity, Kekes observes in his 1996 book *Against Liberalism.* Some of the greatest works of the human spirit, from Montesquieu's *Spirit of the Laws* to Tocqueville's *Democracy in America*, have been written in this noble tradition. In my view, Kekes doesn't sufficiently acknowledge how the contemporary variant of liberalism is at a far remove from the earlier, richer, and more modest liberalism of Montesquieu and Tocqueville, or, closer to our time, the chastened liberalism of Raymond Aron, Bertrand de Jouvenel, and Isaiah Berlin. But he does correctly show that a blind pursuit of the positive goals of contemporary liberals—in particular, autonomy, distributive justice, and equality—will almost cer-

tainly aggravate many of the evils that liberalism has historically sought to overcome.

Take, as an example, the Rawlsian-liberal concern for
justice. For today's left-liberals, justice entails the redistribution of resources in the pursuit of greater equality, regardless of the merit of present holders or future recipients of
goods. On this outlook, justice as equality must disregard
merit, for we don't "deserve" our genetic or social inheri-
tance. Whether someone works hard, excels at school, or is
a fine athlete, in other words, has little to do with them, and
perhaps everything to do with their milieu or the genetic
lottery that they won or lost at birth. Thus we should ensure,
institutionally, that those lucky enough to succeed only get
to enjoy their rewards *after* those unlucky enough to fail first
benefit.

But as Kekes rightly points out, implementing such "justice"
has counterintuitive—even absurd—consequences. In the up-
side-down Rawlsian universe, a single mother who improves
her lot and that of her children through hard work, thrift, and
discipline would find her somewhat greater resources subject
to redistribution to another single mother who, say, was ad-
dicted to drugs, neglected her children, and refused to work.
Where is the justice in that? Pushed to its limit, this logic
would cause greater suffering, since it rewards socially self-
destructive behavior and penalizes virtue. "In deeming this
blatant injustice just," Kekes writes in an essay quoted earlier,
the Rawlsian liberal "repudiates the conception—accepted
from the Old Testament to recent times—that justice consists
in giving people what they deserve: reward for good conduct
and punishment for bad."

Similarly questionable is the liberal emphasis on autonomy—the idea that the self is to be the sole arbiter of its destiny.
Kekes sees autonomy as the god to which all other liberal al-

legiances pay respect. But why should more autonomy mean less evil, as liberals claim? It would only mean that if we were to understand human nature, as Rousseau did, as intrinsically good, and evil to be a mirage of unjust social life that will vanish with the overturning of corrupt institutions. Yet this flies in the face of everything we should sensibly know in 2007, after a century of unprecedented violence, about man's nature: that he is capable of good *and* evil, that his soul is divided, that original sin—though Kekes wouldn't use such language—marks him indelibly. To increase human autonomy, whatever its other effects, is therefore also to increase the human capacity for evil; to bridle evil might require limits on human autonomy.

Earlier liberals like Tocqueville and Montesquieu understood liberty to be a civilizational achievement, inseparable from its articulation within a rich world of goods and spiritual bodies that would nurture it. Rawlsian liberals, Kekes says, embrace an empty freedom, where everything—identity, gender, truth—is up for grabs, and where nothing really means anything. The real spiritual father of contemporary liberalism is Jean-Paul Sartre.

Skeptical Conservatism

Kekes suggests that what is worthwhile in liberalism might best be preserved by a conservative pluralism, one that recognizes the incompatibility of human ends, the necessity of difficult trade-offs, and the existence of certain goods—among them, security, civility, and peace—not given much attention or credence by contemporary liberals. His 1997 book *A Case for Conservatism* offers a systematic presentation of that alternative. It is morally serious, argumentative, and filled with good sense. It is also troubling.

The central concern of conservatism, Kekes explains, is with political arrangements that create the conditions for people to live good lives. Those conditions include, but aren't limited to, civility, equality, freedom, a healthy environment, justice, order, peace, prosperity, rights, security, toleration, and welfare. Conservatives, unlike liberals or socialists, are sensitive to the fragility of political arrangements conducive to good lives, and look to history for lessons on how to nourish and protect them. As Kekes tells it, conservative political morality, growing out of this historical reflection, has four basic components: skepticism, pluralism, traditionalism, and pessimism. Each is an Aristotelian mean between two rejected alternatives.

Conservative skepticism, for instance, encourages a healthy distrust of the two forms of the "nightmare of reason": the rationalist dream of reconstructing reality to make it fit the "latest metaphysical or utopian certainties," and the "fideist" spurning of reason in favor of irrational enthusiasms, whether religious or nationalist in inspiration. Kekes's skepticism leads conservatives "to be cautious in accepting reasons, to want reasons to be concrete, tried, and true, attested to by experience, without pretending to a quixotic pose of the wholesale rejection of the effort to be as reasonable as possible." In an era torn by rationalist and irrationalist political experiments that exacted an immense toll in human suffering, a skeptical attitude—toward political arrangements, anyway—is surely reasonable.

Pluralism is the second component of conservative political morality. Kekes is indebted here to Berlin, the political philosopher who returned repeatedly to the problem posed by the incommensurability of human goods. Berlin argued that a society cannot maximize all good things all at once: there are always trade-offs between, say, liberty and equality or privacy and public spirit. Kekes agrees, and sees pluralism as a via media between absolutism and relativism. Absolutists declare that there is but one good form that all lives must struggle to approximate; relativists proclaim that good lives are just what each society, or perhaps each individual, say they are. Pluralists, Kekes suggests, are more sensibly awake to the variety of political arrangements, conditions, traditions, and conceptions of the good life that human nature legitimately allows. But they are aware, too, that this variety isn't infinite, and that some societies are beyond the pale—evil, in a word.

Kekes devotes a fascinating chapter of his 2005 book *The Roots of Evil* to Robespierre and the Jacobins, whose fanaticism anticipated twentieth-century totalitarianism and was indeed beyond the pale. Kekes unsparingly details the atrocities of Robespierre's two-year reign: women raped, children killed or mutilated, prisoners disemboweled before howling mobs. What licensed the brutality was the Jacobins' ideological approach to politics. Robespierre and his followers, like left-wing revolutionaries ever since, divided the political world in absolute terms. "All political choices of the time were interpreted as choices between morality and immorality, good and evil, virtue and vice," writes Kekes. "The choices Robespierre favored were of course on the side of the angels, so his opponents could be demonized." To illustrate this chilling logic, Kekes offers the words of St. Just, Robespierre's close ally: "The republic consists in the extermination of everything that opposes it."

But is it right to call Robespierre evil, his apologists ask? Wasn't he seeking a better, fairer society? Kekes will have none of it. "Robespierre had people lynched, buried alive, hacked to pieces, slowly drowned, publicly humiliated, and parts of their still-warm bodies devoured by the mob," he observes. Whatever justification one might offer "cannot even begin to account for the savage, inhuman cruelty and ferocious malevolence" of his actions. Even if it *were* necessary to kill his victims—not that it was, of course—the wild excess of the harm he and the Jacobins inflicted reveals the moral truth: pluralism has limits.

Conservatives are also traditionalists, Kekes explains. Like Michael Oakeshott, Kekes defends traditions because they carry tacit knowledge, various excellences, and resources for building meaningful lives. Where tradition runs dry, human impoverishment follows; a strong society will harbor many traditions. A social world "thick" with traditions, Kekes believes, is better than a liberal one devoted to individual autonomy, since autonomy by itself leaves us sad and empty. As Pierre Manent (whose thought we will examine in the next chapter) puts it, what's the worth of choice if choice is all there is? A social world thick with traditions is also better than one where political authority forces traditions into authorized shapes, as the Jacobins attempted, not to mention one in which it is thoroughly obliterated, as in the Soviet Union, which crushed civil society with all the weight that its merciless centralized power could muster.

The final component of conservative political morality is pessimism. Pessimism leads conservatives to reject the "Enlightenment faith" in human perfectibility shared by liberals and socialists. Evil and contingency stain all human affairs. Yet conservatives don't go to the opposite extreme of viewing human nature as irredeemably corrupt. Even in thoroughly evil societies there are instances of acts of decency, generosity, and sacrifice. Pessimism acknowledges both the angel and the brute in man's constitution.

These four components of conservative political morality—skepticism, pluralism, traditionalism, and pessimism—

apply flexibly to three different levels of the human world, Kekes contends. The universal level refers to certain minimal constants of human physiology, psychology, and sociality that all good societies must honor. If political arrangements make famine more likely, or cause people to despair of the future, or generate mistrust and worse among neighbors, then conservatives must condemn them. But on the social level, pluralism holds: as between an authoritarian but prosperous and orderly society and a quarrelsome and liberty-loving society, who can say which is better? Finally, on the individual level, there are many different ways of living good lives, and conservatives should tolerate, though not necessarily respect, as much variety as is compatible with social stability.

The Limits of Secular Conservatism

Much of this is indisputably wise, and conservatives of any stripe will have no hesitancy in endorsing it. But I have several criticisms. First, Kekes betrays a secularist bias that makes him unreasonably suspicious of religious conservatives, whom he dismisses as pigheaded absolutists—though, perhaps tellingly, he never identifies any of these absolutists by name. That bias is strikingly displayed in a passage that comes relatively late in *A Case for Conservatism*, when Kekes, to make a case for the distinction between toleration and respect, asks an "unsympathetic" reader what the appropriate response should be to "racists, anti-Semites, creationists, pedophiles, pornographers, and so forth, who live according to their beliefs without violating any required convention." Now, one might find creationism wrong and unscientific, but are creationists really as morally offensive as racists and pedophiles? Elsewhere, Kekes proclaims without argument that we now know that chastity isn't a virtue. But how can "we" be sure that chastity is atavistic, as the Western world confronts rates of adolescent venereal disease, millions of abortions, and sexually jaded fifteen-year olds? Kekes's position requires more than assertion.

All religious orthodoxy appears to him as a kind of mental zombiism, as in this strange passage from *The Roots of Evil*: "Devout Catholics, orthodox Jews, fundamentalist Protestants, or Shiite Muslims . . . are told what to do and they do it. They have not themselves 'designed and thought' of their actions. They do what is expected of them. And if they are in doubt, they ask their superiors or moral authorities, and they tell them."

As a result of his postreligious theoretical position, Kekes's conception of universal human nature remains too limited. Is an argument for the moral superiority of the traditional family, or for the morally problematic nature of certain sexual practices, illegitimately absolutist? In Kekes's conservative pluralism, it seems so. Moral claims of this kind have no claim to be universal. At best, Kekes grants them a second-order status as part of a particular tradition, implying that a Christian who lived his life in the light of the Second Coming and who honored the theological virtues of the New Testament, or a Jew who embraced the Judaic ethics of divine law, couldn't be a conservative—they would be (presumably dangerous) absolutists. But one can be a Christian or a Jew, argue for the universal truth of one's faith and its moral precepts, and still tolerate human practices that fall short of the ideal or admit the often ambiguous, conflictual, and uncertain nature of moral life.

Kekes is an admirable iconoclast in the stultifying universe of contemporary analytic moral and political philosophy, where conservatives, even of Kekes's secular stripe, are a rarity. His lovely, humane writings, through which the spirit of Montaigne moves, offer real insights into our political condition. We should indeed be skeptical of every attempt to solve the political problem once and for all. We should indeed be pluralists, open to the varieties of human flourishing, at least up to a point. We should indeed respect and nourish traditions. And we should indeed be reasonably pessimistic about human nature, without surrendering to hopelessness. But one needn't be a secularist to affirm such views. Theism has more, and perhaps even better, resources for sustaining Kekes's brand of conservatism than he realizes.

10

What Is Democratic Modernity?

Two of the deepest and most provocative efforts to get a fix on our condition—the free and disillusioned condition of liberal modernity—have been elaborated in a series of books and essays written over the past twenty-five years by two brilliant French political thinkers, Marcel Gauchet and Pierre Manent, both associated with the break with Marxism and the radical Left that has characterized Parisian intellectual life in recent years. The themes of their key works overlap in many ways, but as we will see, they ultimately reach very different conclusions.

The Mad and the Republic

In his influential 1961 book *The History of Madness* (at last available in a full-length English translation), Michel Foucault indicted the modern West for its treatment of the "insane." According to Foucault, Western societies, bowing before the Enlightenment idol of Reason, built a theoretical and institutional quarantine against madness. The Cartesian rational mind must not suffer from exposure to irrationality; the madman must not roam freely through town and country as he did during the Middle Ages—a mocking reminder of human mortality and God's infinite wisdom. Instead, Foucault claimed, the Enlightenment authorities threw the insane into cells with other dissidents from the rising bourgeois order: the poor, the criminal, and the licentious. The supposed liberation of the mad during the late eighteenth and early nineteenth century by "alienists" Phillippe Pinel in France and William Tuke in England, he argued, only furthered their exclusion. These reformers herded the mad into asylums, where an arid and inhuman "science" of psychiatry silenced their Dionysian voices. Such was the price of Reason's "progress."

Though many scholars have questioned its historical accuracy, Foucault's anathema proved a major influence on the anti-psychiatry movement, whose legacy of deinstitutionalization of the insane we still live with today, and it remains a much-taught text in the contemporary university. Marcel Gauchet's first major work, *Madness and Democracy: The Modern Psychiatric Universe*, cowritten with psychiatrist Gladys Swain and published in 1980, took aim at Foucault's history—and its underlying antimodern philosophical premises.

When the publisher Gallimard released the original edition of Gauchet and Swain's book, Foucault agreed to review it for several major publications. He then neglected to write any reviews, assuring the book a muted initial reception. Foucault's biographer claims that the philosopher was intimidated. It's easy to see why. Gauchet and Swain offer a rich historical analysis of the birth of the asylum and the development of psychiatry that is sharply at odds with Foucault's dark approach. Though not uncritical of modern psychiatry (or, for that matter, of the Enlightenment and the modern world), Gauchet and Swain are sober in their conclusions—far removed from Foucault's romantic excesses.

Gauchet, editor of the prestigious intellectual journal *Le Debat* and a director of studies at the École des hautes études en sciences sociales, and Swain, who died at the age of forty-eight in 1995, shine a Tocquevillian light on the historical emergence of psychiatry and the insane asylum, revealing them as inseparable from the development of modern democracy. In articulating the social history of insanity, the authors divide Western political history into three broad eras: the premodern, theocratic universe; democratic modernity; and something new, only now opening before us, which I would call a humbled modernity.

In premodern societies, the mad were indeed free to wander about, just as Foucault claimed; the religiously ordered world of the Middle Ages reserved a place for the insane, as it did for every other creature in God's Great Chain of Being. Yet toleration of the mad did not mean society considered them fully human or that their lot was enviable. On the contrary, mocked and derided, often displayed for public amusement or chased through the streets by cruel children, the insane inhabited the margins of the premodern world—a world of natural hierarchy and exclusion rather than of equality and inclusion. These were creatures "set apart in their differences," say Gauchet and Swain. Reasoning beings had nothing in common with them.

Democratic modernity—Gauchet and Swain's second era—changed everything. Shattering the Great Chain of Being, refounding society on the basis of the social contract, remaking everything in man's image, and unleashing a powerful wave of equality that has yet to crest, modern democratic societies transfigured the status of the mad. The authors credit Pinel and his ally Jean-Etienne Esquirol—the two French fathers of "moral treatment" (i.e., psychiatry) and the asylum—for this new attitude. Contrary to Foucault, who dismissed "moral treatment" as an insidious form of segregation, Gauchet and Swain convincingly show that the new approach expressed confidence in the possibility of communicating with the insane, signaling, for the first time in Western history, that the mad were in some important sense human beings like us, with the capacity to reason. The reach of democratic equality, in other words, now extended to the insane.

Pinel and Esquirol, working in the immediate aftermath of the French Revolution, were initially optimistic about curing the insane and making them full citizens through moral treatment. After all, what was not possible for Revolutionary Man, in full possession of himself and his society? But the alienists' optimism quickly faded. Most of the mad remained stubbornly deranged and often dangerous after treatment. It soon became evident to Pinel and Esquirol that long-term institutional care was unavoidable.

As asylums opened across Europe in the nineteenth century, the goal of moral treatment began subtly to shift from that of seeking a cure to that of socialization. The idea was to get the mad patient to fit in with a more or less permanent population of the insane, to set up a perfectly ordered counter-society of the mad. The asylum became a kind of democratic utopia, cut off from the rest of the world and programmed by psychiatrists as if men—even madmen—were machines, which one could manipulate and plug into the collective. Like all utopias, it didn't work. The human parts resisted their incorporation.

Indeed, the asylum was, Gauchet and Swain suggest, "a sort of laboratory of power" in which the entire trajectory of modern politics played itself out in microcosm, from the naïve faith in human reason born of the democratic revolution, to utopian hopes that one could mold human beings into any shape one desired, to the dismal failure of those hopes. Despite marking a humanitarian advance—one that Foucault's wholesale condemnation of the modern world did not acknowledge—the history of the asylum also prefigured the totalitarian impulse that the democratic universe has carried with it from the start.

But the asylum's strange and unfortunate story points toward a third era of political history, whose outline only now is coming into focus: a humbled modernity. Gauchet and Swain draw two central lessons for this new political order from the asylum's history. The first is what the authors term the "impossibility" of totalitarianism. Projects of total control, from the nineteenth-century asylum to the Khmer Rouge's effort to send Cambodia back to the year zero, have failed repeatedly over the last two centuries, though, as we've noted on several occasions in this volume, not without horrific consequences. They fail because the human being, marked by an "indomitable inventiveness," isn't a machine—and we shouldn't treat him as one. As Gauchet and Swain explain, "Must we not be sensitive first and foremost to the dimension of impossibility, wherever it is a question of reforming personalities or transforming subjects, whenever we are dealing with the powers of institutions or the integral organization of collective space?"

The failure of the asylum allows us to see the tragic side of human freedom. Gauchet and Swain argue that the new model of insanity helps illuminate the modern sense of the self. Just as the first alienists discovered in the mad a capacity to reason and an ability, however truncated, to act as free agents, so modern men learn to grapple with their divided selves, which strive to achieve autonomy without ever completely succeeding. In both instances, the point is to avoid hubris. We cannot overcome the divided self—not by absolutizing freedom and self-mastery, nor by abolishing human liberty. We are both free and not-free, an uneasy condition that we've yet to come to terms with or truly understand.

So what does this dawning era of humbled modernity, unveiled as a negative image by the asylum, look like? It distrusts any utopian efforts to solve the political problem, though it believes the general democratic drift of the modern world to be just. It's aware of the limits of what the state or any centralized authority can do. It recognizes the deep, impenetrable mystery of the human soul. It has a sense of tragedy. We can see it, I believe, in the abandonment of the most wild-eyed dreams of recreating the human world through politics; in the reorganizations of businesses away from top-down, heavily bureaucratic management structures toward more flexible, decentralized practices; and in our confused, groping steps toward a new approach to the mentally ill that would neither restore the big asylum nor leave the insane to fend for themselves, as did deinstitutionalization.

A Disenchanted World?

Gauchet's *The Disenchantment of the World* (1985) is even more sweeping in its intellectual ambition, offering nothing short of a new theory of the birth of modernity (including the modernity of the asylum) out of the spirit of Christianity. Ranging across religious history, anthropology, political philosophy, sociology, and economics, Gauchet challenges the narrowness of much recent philosophy and places religion at the center of the human condition, where it rightfully belongs.

Gauchet's argument, not always easy to follow through the dense thicket of his prose, is that religion lies at the foundation of the social order, Western political and economic institutions, and our self-understanding. Religion, on Gauchet's view, forms a "counter-subjectivity," an "other" that always exists in relation to human subjectivity. Religion and freedom—the latter understood by the author as man's power to innovate, to liberate himself from the weight of history, and to give himself (recalling Rousseau) his own moral law—oppose one another. Political history tells the long story of religion's withdrawal and the coming into being of a "disenchanted" world, where man, exercising his liberty, is the measure of all things.

The most fully realized forms of religion are not the elaborately developed monotheistic faiths of Judaism, Christianity, or Islam, according to Gauchet, but the "primeval" religions that existed prior to the five millennia of Western history. In these prepolitical societies, lost in time, man experienced radical dispossession: the past determined the laws that regulated every aspect of life. Moreover, the sacred founding of the world was beyond human control, or even questioning. While ritual could reenact the founding, reminding everyone of its inescapability, no one could assume its authority—all were equal before it. But though man had no access to the foundation of the human world, he nevertheless lived in a state of "enchantment," with no clear line dividing the mundane from the realm in which occult forces were at work. In these ancient, magical, egalitarian societies, the gods rumbled through nature, present beside man in an all-encompassing order. For countless ages, the rhythm of life beat slowly, as if the universe slumbered.

"The deepest enigma of history" is at work in these time-lost societies, Gauchet believes, for man's freedom means that he's capable of transcending his circumstances, of altering the earth, his social relations, even his most profound beliefs, according to his will. Strange, then, that primeval religion froze this power in place for tens of thousands of years; perhaps it answered some deep need of human nature. Only with the emergence of the state in ancient Egypt and Mesopotamia, 3,000 years before the birth of Christ—relatively recently when we consider the span of human history—was the rhythm broken, and did we find ourselves "plunged . . . into another religious world, one capable of existing without religion—our own."

What did the state introduce? Structurally, it opened space for human action, since power, after all, exists for people to use. And use it man soon did—to conquer others. Politics entered the world, disrupting the equality that was characteristic of primeval religion; rulers arose who, justifying their elevation from run-of-the-mill mortals, identified themselves with the gods. As politics and religion entwined, the sacred law was no longer completely beyond human reach. Gauchet believes that the major world religions, including prophetic Judaism, grew out of this initial existential fracture.

The world religions of the "Axial Age" (the coinage is philosopher Karl Jasper's) brought with them a three-fold "dynamics of transcendence." First, the sacred, widely dispersed throughout nature, came together in the form of an omnipotent God, acting in the world but increasingly transcendent from it. Second, God's transcendence led man to abandon magical explanations for the phenomena that surrounded him. Third, the idea of human universality spread with the extension of political empire—the new God was to be the God of all men. The dynamics of transcendence result in a fascinating paradox, Gauchet says: the more powerful God becomes, the "more man is free." With monotheism, man began to reason for himself, to question the divine law, to embrace his liberty. The historical process of disenchantment was under way.

Christianity forges a very different relationship between the human and the divine, forming, in Gauchet's arresting phrase, the "religion for departing from religion." At the end of the Christian era, we thus find ourselves at the heart of modernity, entering a postreligious age of human autonomy, democracy, science, and capitalism, with the effective truth of Christianity unveiled as secularism.

How does Christianity bring about the disenchantment of the world? Typically, whether we trace the onset of modernity to Machiavelli (as does Leo Strauss), or to Descartes (as does the Italian Catholic thinker Augusto Del Noce), it is seen, at least in its main path, as a divorce from Christianity. Was not the Catholic Church, in the eyes of the great Enlightenment thinkers, the sworn enemy of reason, human freedom, and the panoply of goods we associate too exclusively with the modern world?

But for Gauchet, modernity grew within Christianity, the result of the inner logic of the faith working itself out historically. Far from opposing one another, Christianity and modernity are historically inseparable—in fact, viewed from Gauchet's Olympian perspective, they're one and the same phenomenon. Voltaire's *Ecrasez l'infame* becomes the cry of a confused Christian.

Though related claims issued forth from Feuerbach in the nineteenth century, and more recently from figures as diverse as Karl Lowith and Harvey Cox, Gauchet's analysis is original in its reliance on political anthropology and sociology, whereas his predecessors wrote in an essentially philosophical or theological idiom. Moreover, Gauchet emphasizes that the disenchantment of the world is not synonymous with progress, as Feuerbach and others would have it, but merely a movement toward one pole of the human world, that of autonomy—no more rational a solution to the problem of being in the world than is the pole of dispossession in leaves behind.

Various elements within Christianity, in Gauchet's telling, lead to its undoing: (1) Christ's incarnation that God was willing to sacrifice his only Son for this finite reality—gave greater dignity to this world than it had ever received from any other source; (2) Christ's appearance in history meant that no political leader could presume to incarnate the divine, creating the conceptual space needed for political liberty; (3) the Son of Man, a simple carpenter, occupied the bottom of the social hierarchy, sowing the seed of human equality; (4) the Christian emphasis on conscience destabilized faith by opening everything to social and individual questioning, making way for philosophical liberalism; and (5) the complete transcendence of the Christian God forced men to take responsibility for themselves where God's voice seemed silent, leading to a kind of "terrestrial integrity," the ejection of all magic from the world, and hence also the birth of modern science. Christianity nourishes a community of autonomous men with no need for God. Eventually, these Christian ideas, outgrowing their religious "superstructure" (Gauchet uses the Marxist concepts of base and superstructure but inverts their meaning), led to the discrediting of religion and the creation of democratic, individualist, and very human societies.

The Disenchantment of the World concludes with a section titled "Figures of the Human Subject," which depicts postreligious modern man. Some people may still believe in God, explains Gauchet, and even be profoundly religious, but this is a private faith, as each person seeks what religion can do for him—hence the proliferation of New Age spiritualities. A religious believer in a democratic society like the United States, who can choose what to believe from a bazaar of traditional and nontraditional beliefs, already inhabits a postreligious landscape. The relationship to the past at the core of primitive religions winds up reversed in the modern world. Deaf to the call of his predecessors, man now organizes his cultural, economic, and political institutions solely with the present and future in view. The law of reality is no longer repetition, but creation—and so we have the vertiginous agitation of our productive capitalist societies, making today what is obsolete tomorrow.

But the Enlightenment ideal of perfect human autonomy proves illusory. Instead of obeying the other outside of us, as in the religious era, we rediscover it within, in the unconscious, rendering our own identity opaque. Instead of our desires, wants, and principled beliefs finding perfect representation in the democratic general will, we discover in our political and economic life something outside of and distinct from what we sought. As Gauchet's two major books on the French Revolution—*La Révolution des droits de l'homme* (1989) *and La Révolution des pouvoirs* (1995)—show, conflict is at the heart of our democratic politics; any effort to overcome that essential pluralism, whether in an attempt to restore some mythic national community or to forge a future radical utopia, will bring totalitarianism. Our societies explode with individualist demands that only the state answers, so (despite what libertarians say) the more we loosen our morals, the more the state expands. Following the great French liberal Benjamin Constant, Gauchet sees man as perpetually dissatisfied and ironic. Wisdom lies in recognizing that no perfect solution to the human problem exists.

Gauchet's "political history of religion" thus culminates in a disenchanted liberalism, aware of its failings but convinced that no other viable prospect is now on offer. There's much to admire in Gauchet's retelling of Western history. An atheist, he is surprisingly aware that we cannot understand the Western experience without taking Christianity seriously. Indeed, he treats Christianity with more respect than do many progressive Christians. A modern liberal, he acknowledges the imperfections and existential limits of liberalism more readily than did, say, John Rawls. With all this, one can have sympathy. But finally, his effort fails.

It fails, I think, for two reasons, one historical, the other a problem of human agency, though the first is related to the second. Gauchet's interpretation of modernity doesn't do justice either to the founders of modernity or to those Christians who resisted it. By describing the modern world as the inexorable working out of certain ideas, reflected in our attitudes about the mad or in Christian institutions and beliefs, ideas that moderns and Christians supposedly were not fully conscious that they held, Gauchet undersells the radical *project* of modernity. We see this project in the brazen contempt for Christianity displayed by Machiavelli in his *Discourses on Livy,* and we see it in Hobbes's attempt, in *Leviathan*, to build an artificial political authority based on the individual free from the demands of nature and grace. These men and those who followed them weren't simply dancing to the orders of a structural choreographer, a sort of Christian social subconscious existing offstage. They knew what they were doing, and they knew it keenly. The modern world was at least partly *thought* before it became a *reality*. Gauchet's anthropological reading of Western history sometimes seems to refuse to take agency seriously.

Perhaps this is why Gauchet, for all the reflection he devotes to Christianity, never considers that Christianity might be true, and that Christians might believe rationally because Jesus Christ revealed the meaning of history two millennia ago. As the philosopher Charles Taylor has noted, Gauchet's anthropological perspective on religion risks reading like "Hamlet without the Prince." The Christian emphasis on conscience, for example, appears in a very different light if Christ indeed brought the truth—since the truth calls to man's freedom, and without truth, his freedom is incomplete, or is no freedom at all.

We Moderns

One finds a more satisfactory account of the origins and consequences of modernity in the work of Pierre Manent, a former assistant to Raymond Aron and today, like his friend and occasional interlocutor Gauchet, a director of studies at the École des hautes études en sciences sociales. In writings of astonishing philosophical depth, Manent has sought to illuminate our past, present, and future in the hope that, suitably armed with knowledge, we might better preserve the legitimate goods that liberal democracy has achieved, while ameliorating, to the extent possible, the evils that those goods have brought with them. Unlike Gauchet, he understands that modernity was a project, rather than a process.

Manent's initial impulse in investigating the "modern difference"–the idea, central to the architects of the modern state, that man could re-found the world based on reason–leads us back in Western political history to the period following the Roman empire's collapse. In *An Intellectual History of Liberalism* (1987), his second major work, Manent argues that the true trajectory of liberal modernity only becomes clear against the backdrop of the "theological-political" problem that Europeans confronted in the wake of Roman decline.

At that time in history, a series of political "forms" was available for the peoples of Europe. Two possibilities suggested themselves immediately, even naturally, to the European: empire and the city-state. The first, Manent explains, mirrored the universality of human nature–the natural impulse to bring together all that might properly range itself under the term "human"; the second built a stage upon which man could control "his conditions of existence through human association." Yet despite long historical precedent, neither political form took root as Europe's history got underway.

The reason lies in the role played by a third form: the Catholic Church. The church posed two difficulties for Europe, the first merely circumstantial, the second, far more importantly, growing out of the institution's very self-definition. With the barbarian invasions ravaging Europe, the church, as the strongest standing institution, found itself performing social and political tasks that normally were the province of political authorities. This shift in responsibilities had the obvious result of temporarily blurring the line between the sacred and the profane, or of mixing secular and religious functions.

The second difficulty, which Manent calls "structural," goes much deeper. The good that the church offers is supernatural: the ultimate good of salvation. While in principle leaving the realm of Caesar to Caesar, the church's commitment to that good gives it, at least in its self-conception, "a right or duty to oversee everything that could place this salvation in peril," writes Manent. In other words, by its very nature the church is led to assert a right to governance over the entire constellation of human activity, including the most significant activity of all—political life. The church thus found itself drawn to claim supreme power over the human world. The Catholic Church at once left man free to organize this world as he saw fit and, paradoxically, tended to impose its own rule. The remarkable tension between the universal empire claimed by the church and the distance it established from concrete political institutions made the church the ultimate threat to the autonomy of the secular universe. At the same time, it created the conceptual and institutional space for political resistance to its dominion.

What political form would be strong enough, at the heart of the theological-political problem, to resist the church's power and ensure the secular world's independence? The city-state was too weak, too particular, to do so for long. And the church had co-opted the empire's claim to universality by more successfully instantiating a universal community. What emerged as an effective response to this fraught situation . was the absolute or national monarchy—a form less particular than the city-state (and thus not as weak), but one whose claim to universality wasn't so easily co-opted. The western European monarch set himself, and history, on the path toward establishing the secular city, the City of Man.

The construction of the *civitas hominum* required a transformation in Western man's spiritual and political order comparable with few others in history. We usually refer to this transformation as modernity, and, following Leo Strauss, Manent locates its first philosophical moment in Machiavelli. With Machiavelli, one no longer looked at political life from the perspective of its end, as in classical thought, but from the standpoint of its often-violent foundation. Politics was no longer the cultivation of the goods intrinsic to man's political nature. Instead, it became a laboratory in which the "alchemy of evil" might occur—in which fear and evil held sway over human destiny. Those wanting to see, and see truly, the political world must "go to the effectual truth of the thing," Machiavelli advised, which teaches us that "a man who wants to make a profession of good in all regards must come to ruin among so many who are not good."

Anticipated by Machiavelli's political science, which granted complete autonomy to a politics divorced from the good, absolute monarchy found its most important theorist in Thomas Hobbes. The matrix for Hobbes's remodeling of the social order was the individual, an artificial construct that has helped drive the subsequent movement of Western history, tending "more and more to become a reality." The Hobbesian individual, anxious in the state of nature, exists prior to the claims that the earthly city or the church make upon him. These claims oriented politics toward the good, either natural or supernatural. In each case, the good equated itself with human ends that the laws had to inscribe if they were to find realization. The Hobbesian vision saw in these claims not the realization of human nature, but rather the source of human suffering, represented for Hobbes by the English Civil War:

> And as to Rebellion in particular against the Monarchy; one of the most frequent causes of it, is the reading of the books of Policy, and Histories of the antient Greeks, and Romans; from which, young men, and all others that unprovided of the Antidote of solid Reason, receiving a strong, and delightfull impression, of the great exploits of warre, atchieved by the Conductors of their Armies, receive withall a pleasing Idea, of all they have done besides; and image their great prosperity, not to have proceeded from the aemulation of particular men, but from the virtue of their popular forme of government: Not considering the frequent Seditions, and Civill warres, produced by the imperfection of their Policy.

Both the classical notion of nature and the assurance of having grace led to the arrogance of superiority, or of the elect; both democratic demands and ecclesiastical presumption needed taming. Yet if their conflicting, incommensurable conceptions of the good tear men apart, Hobbes reasoned, they can agree on something primordial: fear of death. In the state of nature, the sheer force of this passion renders men equal.

Manent urges us to attend closely to this extremely important moment in the history of Western intellectual life.

Hobbesian man finds his primordial right in the need he has to survive—a need that he feels with the force of necessity when there is no state, or when the state is unable to secure the conditions of civil peace, as in Iraq today. Hobbes's state of nature is the image of the internal contradictions that riddled the classical and Christian traditions, "the final realization of the factional disorders of the Greek cities as much as the wars of religion known by the Christian world," as Manent puts it in perhaps his most ambitious book, *The City of Man* (1994).

More, the contradictions weren't just internal to each tradition, but grew out of their reciprocal critique: "since the city and the church reproach one another with the vanity of their sacrifice," Manent points out, "the individual is he who refuses each form of sacrifice, and who defines himself by this refusal. From each tradition, the individual accepts the critique that it makes of the other, and concludes that he never is obliged to die, nor to suffer, that in fact the right to live is the foundation and totality of his moral being." The individual—again, prior to any law or moral demand, whether the magnanimity of the Greek or the humility of the saint—will be central to modern man's self-consciousness.

Hobbes taught a harsh lesson: nature is not good, and a life lived according to nature is ultimately unlivable. The evils of natural existence aren't rooted in sin, however, but in necessity. Such evils require healing by art, not by the grace of Christ. The artificial authority that men agree to build, the mighty Leviathan, uses its power to make men fear it more than each other in order to establish civil peace. (Michael Oakeshott called this a "homeopathic" remedy to the state of nature.) Otherwise, it ignores the states of souls. The basic needs of individuals, and their willed consent, henceforth provide the foundation for political legitimacy. "Men must no longer be guided by goods or the good, but by the right that is born from the necessity of fleeing evil," Manent writes. "In the moral and political language developed by Hobbes, and which is still ours today, the *right* replaces the *good*. The intensity of moral approval that the ancients gave to the good, the moderns, following Hobbes, gave to the right, the right of the individual. This is the language and 'value' of liberalism."

The individual will live in a "third city," where he belongs neither to the natural world of the earthly city nor to the city of God. The history of modern society is about the desire to flee the political power of revealed religion. It is also about the new difficulties posed by the elaborate machine erected to satisfy this desire: the agnostic modern state. Three major modern thinkers–Locke, Montesquieu, and Rousseau–help Manent model the "major articulations" of the liberal democratic regime.

Locke. Locke makes the idea of representation, along with property, the pith of this political thinking. This notion, as Manent suggests, was a response to the danger that Hobbes's Leviathan posed to the newborn individual it was supposed to protect. But Locke's emphasis on the legislative sphere, the natural home of the representative, fails in turn adequately to think through the problem of the executive. In *An Intellectual History of Liberalism*, Manent leads us, in a close reading of Locke, to acknowledge both the importance and the troubling nature of the strong executive in modern liberal societies. This executive is not an atavism from the monarchical period but rather a necessary part of the functioning of liberal regimes. Without a strong executive–a de Gaulle, Churchill, Thatcher, Reagan, or Giuliani–liberal societies can lose what Manent has called "the instinct for political existence." The centripetal forces of civil society then transform men into mere confederates, as opposed to citizens.

Montesquieu. Montesquieu teaches the separation of powers, another key liberal doctrine, where social "outcomes" aren't the result of consciously sought goods but instead a by-product of mutual prevention. I stop you from getting exactly what you want. You keep me from my true desire. A third, unintended, outcome follows. Manent relies on Montesquieu to explore the ceaseless upheaval of liberal societies. The often banal but prosperous materialism that surrounds us in a commercial society, defusing more dangerous political ideals, has its most articulate defense in Montesquieu's examination of the English Constitution in *The Spirit of the Laws.* (This may be why Manent enigmatically refers to Montesquieu in *The City of Man* as "the modern philosopher most capable of losing us as well as saving us.")

Rousseau. In the paradoxical figure of Rousseau, liberalism meets its most brilliant critic. Rousseau excoriates the bourgeois individual whom Montesquieu so ably defends: he is cut off from his responsibility and power as citizen. Rousseau's response to the weakness of modern man was not to propose some return to classical modes of thought about nature; it was to encourage a farther flight from nature—a radicalization of human liberty. The only limits to autonomy should come from autonomous men; on such a basis a new civic spirit would arise on the terrain of modernity. Manent shows how, with Rousseau, modern political thought reaches its limit—the connection to nature finally is severed completely. What remains: history, freedom, and the end of political philosophy. Once history replaces the idea of nature, there can no longer be deliberation about the best regime—the one that conforms most to man's nature.

Manent's interpretation of modernity owes something to Strauss's. But Manent believes that Strauss doesn't sufficiently account for the radicalism of the break with the past. Nor does Strauss adequately explain why the modern movement has accelerated, constituting a "movement ever more in motion," as Manent put it in a 1994 essay in the French journal *Commentaire*. In Manent's view, one must take seriously the ancient, modern, and *Christian* sources of the modern movement. After the horrors of the French Revolution, liberalism took a more critical, even pessimistic turn in the nineteenth century. Benjamin Constant, François Guizot, and, most importantly, Alexis de Tocqueville all wrote with the Terror in view. It is in Tocqueville that we find the richest formulation of the problem of liberal democratic societies, and the most vivid description of the direction toward which they—we—are heading. As Manent suggests at the beginning of his 1982 study *Tocqueville and the Nature of Democracy*, the French aristocrat, dead for over two centuries, helps "explain us to ourselves." What did Tocqueville see?

The Mirror of Democracy

Tocqueville, in Manent's reading, brings to light three questions central to grasping the meaning of liberal modernity: What is the nature of democracy, the natural fruit of liberalism? What effects does it have on the nature of man? What must we do to defend its achievements and mitigate its worst tendencies?

Tocqueville arrived on American shores in May 1831, seeking clarity about the essence of democracy, which was obscured from view in Europe by the disruptions of the French Revolution. The journey gave birth, of course, to *Democracy in America*. In America, Tocqueville could observe with an unimpeded view the democratic revolution working itself out. And what was the primordial fact of democracy? It was the equality of conditions, a social state in which the influence of one individual over another—central to the aristocratic regime—gives way to the egalitarian idea of individual consent. "In such a society," Manent explains, "the acts of each have only two legitimate sources: personal will or the general will." The victory of consent over all influences has dramatic social, political, and moral effects. Tocqueville was filled with a religious dread when faced with this historical mutation, which he saw as providential.

It's worth briefly considering some of the examples Tocqueville used to illustrate the democratic transformation in history; they will be familiar to any one of us from our daily lives. Democracy has substantially modified intellectual life, Tocqueville believed. Under pressure from the individual, opinions become relativized, mores softened. Public opinion emerges as the sole authoritative voice. What one might call the tyranny of tolerance, or a refusal of the responsibility of judgment, finds a home in the human world. As for the modification of human passions, while individual rights govern the lives of men, the ends of men continue their long fall—begun, as we've seen, in Machiavelli's time—into neglect. What Manent refers to as the "moral contents of life" pour out of the liberal democratic vessel. The family, religion, virtues—the democratic "contract" remakes them all. The passion for equality, natural to democracy, trumps every other concern, and begins its endless struggle to eradicate the natural inequalities of men.

Tocqueville's mirror reflects back at us a tragic, and indeed paradoxical, truth: democracy is both natural to man and, if not moderated, destructive of human nature. Allowed free reign, this passion for equality, which is a kind of democratic instinct, undermines democracy itself. It does so in several ways: by re-creating the state of nature, originally elaborated by Hobbes, Locke, and Rousseau as a pre-civilized condition, at the heart of democratic society; by spreading envy, corrosive of any regime; and by crowding out all natural superiorities, whether those of reason or those of virtue. Though Tocqueville believed the aristocratic regime to be unjust, based as it was on an unnatural convention of familial superiority, its hierarchical order still preserved room for standards that transcended the individual will. The excellences of human nature had, at least potentially and for the few, room to breathe. The democratic regime threatens to eliminate every reference point beyond the sovereign individual. When this occurs, Tocqueville fretted, democracy, at least in its liberal form, would run aground. We will no longer seek the true, the good, and the beautiful, and our institutions will begin to weaken.

The "democratic man" is, as Tocqueville captures him, a strange creature: clamoring for rights, uncertain of his beliefs, obsessed with material gain (the only thing he can be certain of), anxious, solitary, and mediocre. His various defects make him prey for the "soft" despotism that Tocqueville so dreaded, under which liberty is lost and a bloated central power administers to the needs of an infantilized population. Central to Tocqueville's purpose was to avoid a future in which this soft despotism would triumph. Yet no simple return to aristocracy was possible:

> On the one hand, democracy's project is unrealizable, because it is contrary to nature. On the other, it is impossible to stop short of this democracy and go back to aristocracy. This is because democratic equality also conforms to nature. It follows that we can only moderate democracy; we cannot stop short of democracy, because it fulfills nature. We cannot attain the end of this movement, for it would mean subjecting nature

completely and dehumanizing man. We cannot escape
democracy. We can never make democracy completely
"real," and we must not try. We can and must moderate
democracy, limit it, temper its hostility to nature, all
the while benefiting from its conformity to nature. To
affirm and will democracy insofar as it is in conformity
with nature, to limit it insofar as it is contrary to it, such
is the sovereign art on which depend the prosperity and
morality of democracies.

Time and again, Manent argues that democracy is silent
on the most important question: what is man? It can provide
no coherent answer to those who, for reasons of efficiency or
malevolence or misplaced sympathy, want to dispose of society's weakest members—the aged and the unborn, the mar-
ginal and the powerless. It can provide no real foundation
for the creation of beauty. It's response to truth and falsity
is solely pragmatic. Therefore we must, in Manent's words,
love democracy "moderately." It does not deserve our absolute devotion.

Moderating Modernity

Can a modern regime like America's, which is in some
ways based on the flight from substantive conceptions of
the good, find the resources to preserve itself? Or are all
modern regimes, as Rocco Buttiglione fears, at risk of com-
mitting suicide? In his most directly political book, *A World
beyond Politics?* (2001), Manent tries to provide an "impartial overview of the political order—or disorder—of today's
world."

The bourgeois order, Manent forthrightly acknowledges—
and anyone who reads his work will see that he is no antimod-

ern reactionary—has offered "the most stable, therefore the most satisfying putting into practice of political liberty that humanity has ever known." But because it separates power from opinion, especially religious opinion, the liberal regime frustrates a natural instinct to see our highest ideals reflected in political life. It is, in this sense, permanently dissatisfying. Like Gauchet, Manent believes that the liberal order invites utopian efforts to replace it with a pure "politics of meaning." The two deadliest threats to liberal democracy—communism and National Socialism—were hyperpolitical projects of this kind, Manent says. The Islamist terrorists who struck on 9/11 represent another.

A subtler threat to liberal democracy seeks to leave politics behind entirely, to embody a universal civilization of pure rights or commerce. Manent sees this postpolitical trend at work in the European Union, at least in its current form. Aristotle described citizenship as an act of putting forth words and deeds in a common space. But Europeans don't know what they share in that common space: they forge new shared institutions but leave the old national ones still in place, creating a bizarre "juxtaposition of old and new institutions" that guarantees maximum confusion and political alienation. Even the EU's territorial boundaries—essential to all forms of politics—remain blurry. Should the EU include Turkey? Russia? Where does one draw the line? Who's the boss?

Manent believes that the EU project is, in its own way, as utopian as the twentieth-century totalitarianisms. To be real, democracy "needs a *body*, a population marked out by borders and other characteristics, namely a *defined* realm." The nation-state, discredited in Europe by the brutality of mega-lomaniacal nationalism—gave democracy a body. Europe's dream of tossing the nation into the dustbin of history is understandable, given the history of the twentieth century. But what "political form" takes its place? Unless the EU becomes a kind of United States of Europe, with clear territorial limits and a will to act politically—so far utterly missing except when it is thwarting the United States—its woolly, confused nature ensures collapse. The EU's antipolitical drift is most evident in its hallucinatory belief that war is obsolete and that all conflict can give way to rational negotiation and consensus. The lessons of history—including Europe's own recent history in the Balkans—tell otherwise. (Manent returns to these themes in his most recent book, *La raison des nations*, published in 2006.)

A defining feature of our societies for Manent, as we've seen, is to make man "the sovereign author, in fact and by right, of the human world." Not so long ago, one got up in the morning, looked around, and saw bonds everywhere: one's mother-in-law lived, if not under one's own roof, then right next door; the church explained what one ought to do; everywhere there were duties, duties, duties. This moral density defined men and women, shaped their lives. It could also be a burden, of course. The "logic" of democracy, as Manent calls it, loosened these thick attachments—and hasn't stopped loosening them. "Democracy aims to have its citizens go from a life that one suffers, receives, and inherits to a life that one wills. Democracy makes all relations and all bonds voluntary." Pushed to excess, this process culminates in a Sartrean existentialism, where nothing—not even my own voluntary agreements, like, say, my marriage—means anything unless, right now, this instant, it means something to me. All that is solid melts into air, as the saying goes.

Still, this nihilism is only a tendency of modern life, not a fate. The old order was not as oppressive to liberty as sometimes thought: Marriage in Christian Europe, for instance, always rested on the principle of consent. Similarly, it remains possible to create thick attachments in our free societies. "In the new democratic order, free personal searching is now a right but it can lead to deep and lasting adherences, whether it be the formation of a couple or participation in a religious or other type of community." Ordered liberty isn't out of date. And we all still argue, fortunately, about right and wrong ways to live; just look at any political discussion group on the Web.

The prudential "art" of democracy, Manent advises, is to correct for the relativizing tendencies of democratic modernity—and to do so without succumbing to the potentially abusive temptation to prop up any one experience or worldview as civically absolute. A healthy democratic politics is vital in this regard. Such a politics "prevents any experience from saturating the social arena and the individual consciousness; it requires any experience to coexist and communicate with the other experiences. In this way, politics is the guardian of the wealth and complexity of human life." There is in Manent a classical sense of politics as architectonic, and of human nature as in some sense political.

In addition to a healthy sense of national belonging and a robust democratic politics, Manent (a believing Catholic) also believes that religion, playing a transpolitical role, can moderate the excesses of liberal modernity. Catholicism, if it can at once accommodate itself to democratic political institutions and resist pressures itself to become a democratic body, can instill vital spiritual energies into our social order by pointing beyond the individual. In an essay published during the 1990s, Manent argued that the Catholic Church possesses a "dialectical advantage" over democracy in that it carries with it a clear teaching on the meaning and destiny of man.

Finally—and here Manent's thought recalls that of Allan Bloom, or, in a different idiom, John Kekes—a renewed commitment to classical education can help us escape our democratic prejudices. Education should direct us beyond ourselves. It should open up vistas where the goods of our nature once again become recognizable—if only in an aesthetic or imaginary way. Without such a connection with our past, however tenuous, we surrender to the modern tide of historical becoming.

There is no recipe or equation in all of this. We need no ideologies, no programs. But analyses like Manent's raise the possibility that by connecting with our preliberal past, we might find our way toward a genuinely postliberal—as opposed to antiliberal—future.

Index

About the Author

Brian C. Anderson is the editor of *City Journal*, the cultural and political quarterly published by the Manhattan Institute, where he writes extensively on social and political trends. Aside from his articles in *City Journal*, his work has appeared in the *Wall Street Journal*, the *Los Angeles Times*, the *New York Post*, *National Review*, and the *Weekly Standard*, among many other publications. Anderson is also the author of *South Park Conservatives* and *Raymond Aron: The Recovery of the Political*.